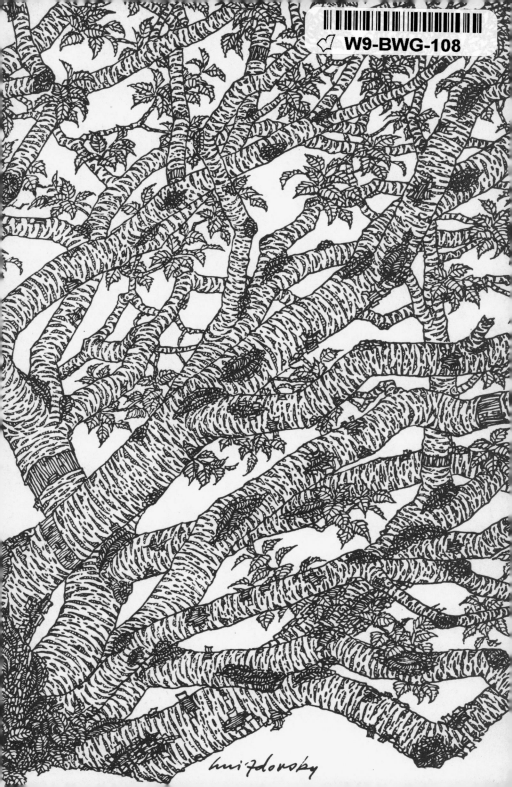

TREE TRAILS
in
CENTRAL PARK

by

M. M. GRAFF

ILLUSTRATED BY JACQUES HNIZDOVSKY

GREENSWARD FOUNDATION, INC.

New York   1970

For

HENRY HOPE REED

Historian · Critic · Author

Innovative Leader of Cultural Tours

Throughout Greater New York

Curator and Champion of

Central Park

ACKNOWLEDGMENTS

THE author extends warm thanks to George Kalmbacher and Frederick McGourty, Jr., taxonomists of the Brooklyn Botanic Garden, for invaluable help in establishing identification and in checking the manuscript; to Jacques Hnizdovsky, gifted and generous friend of trees, for the drawings and woodcuts that enrich this book; to Charles Farrell for the typographical design; to Richard Edes Harrison, designer of the informative map of Central Park; and to William Toporcer, whose recollections bring to life the endless joy and adventure of a boyhood in Central Park.

This book was made possible by generous gifts from

Josephine B. Crane Foundation
The J. M. Kaplan Fund, Inc.
John Lindsley Fund
Mrs. Henry L. Moses
Anne S. Richardson Fund

and from an anonymous friend of Central Park as a tribute to the conservation achievements of

Georgianna Hubbard McCabe.

CONTENTS

ILLUSTRATIONS

BEFORE YOU START

Trees in Central Park are like notes in music. If you study them only as individuals, you may miss the deeper harmony, the underlying plan and purpose of the landscape design. The park's history is inseparable from the present but you needn't stand in the park shifting from one foot to the other while you read about it. Especially on the longer tours, it is advisable to get the background material in mind before you start out. You can then move fairly quickly from tree to tree without losing a sense of continuity.

It is essential to follow the tours in sequence. The full list of keys to identification is given the first time a tree is encountered. On subsequent meetings, technical descriptions give way to more casual items of historical interest or entertainment. If you start in the middle, you will find out how Indians made cream from hickory nuts. The information is pointless if you haven't learned to recognize a hickory.

As a primary aid to navigation, you should know that the first two numbers on a lamp post indicate the nearest cross street: #9723 is in line with 97th Street. If the next post you come to is #9614, you will know that you are heading south.

A hand lens—8× or stronger—is indispensable if you want to identify trees with certainty. Without one, you will miss conclusive and often beautiful details: the gradation of color on the bud scales of a red oak, the cockscomb glands on a nannyberry, the minute stubble on an English elm leaf, or the gold-powdered buds of a bitternut hickory. In giving marks of identification, I have included only those that can be seen without breaking or injuring plants.

By the end of the tours, you will have seen and learned to recognize 118 trees and shrubs, not merely as isolated specimens but as integral parts of Olmsted and Vaux's pastoral symphony.

I

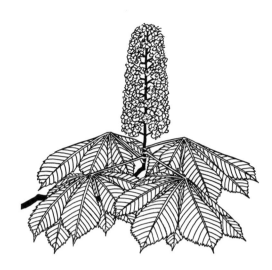

MONTANYE'S RIVULET

100th Street
and Central Park West

THE Pool and its vicinity offer a splendid introduction
to the rich variety of trees in Central Park. Here we
shall meet some of our most majestic native trees in
happy combination with hills, water, and rocks. The
setting evokes the spaciousness and repose of a pastoral
landscape. It represents the highest ideal of urban park
scenery envisioned by Frederick Law Olmsted and Calvert Vaux when they created the prize-winning Greensward plan for Central Park in 1858. The serene
atmosphere of the Pool, unspoiled by structural encroachments, retains the clear imprint of the designers' genius.

As you face the park at 100th Street, take the left-hand path on the north side of the road. The first tree on your left, close to the wall, is a young Osage orange, *Maclura pomifera*. This species was originally found in a small area of Arkansas, Texas, and Oklahoma, the territory of Osage Indians. It is now spread over much of the country, largely because of its usefulness to farmers. When planted as hedges, its thorny branches made cattle-proof enclosures for prairie farms. The wood is exceptionally resistant to rot, even when in contact with the soil, and was favored for fence posts and the supports of frame houses and barns.

Osage orange leaves, dark green and shiny on top and white-fuzzy beneath, are narrow ovals tapering to a long tip, often with a slight twist. The fruit, as much as 5 inches in diameter, is a pebble-surfaced globe, chartreuse in color, and filled with tough fibers, seeds, and acrid juice. The bright orange color of the bark is an unmistakable key to identification, especially in winter when the sun strikes full on the trunk and branches.

To the right of the steps, standing alone, is a horse-chestnut, *Aesculus hippocastanum*, which divides into four trunks about 8 feet above ground. In early May it resembles a giant candelabrum with upright panicles of large white flowers, blotched with crimson and dusted with gold freckles. Flowers are followed by spiky green husks which enclose a shining brown, inedible nut.

This is a compound leafed tree, the first of many to be met on these tours. Simple leaves such as those of oak and maple have a solitary blade on each leafstalk; compound leaves are composed of multiple leaflets. There are two main patterns of compound leaves. One is the palmate leaf in which leaflets radiate from a central point somewhat like the fingers of a hand or the ribs of a palmleaf fan. The other and far more common is the pinnate leaf with leaflets spaced like the barbs of a

2

feather along a central stalk. As you can see, the horse-chestnut has palmate leaves.

Below the horsechestnut, along the edge of the path, are a number of black locusts, *Robinia pseudo-acacia*. Leaves are pinnately compound with small rounded leaflets set along a central leafstalk. The bark of black locusts is an easy means of identification at all seasons: it is medium to dark brown with a pattern of interlacing ridges in high relief. The tree is most decorative in May when its lacy canopy of leaves is hung with profuse clusters of white pea-flowers with a heavenly fragrance, as appealing to bees as to humans.

The wood of black locusts is exceptionally durable in the ground as well as being the strongest of our native trees when used as a beam. Because of these qualities, it is used for timbers in mines and for fence posts as well as for ladder rungs, rake teeth, and policemen's clubs. In the early days of the Colonies, the tough black locust wood was of prime value for wooden nails or dowel pins in shipbuilding. Unfortunately the black locust in many areas is plagued by borers and often disfigured by dead limbs and broken leaders. The tree nearest us seems to have escaped borer damage as it is unusually tall and well formed.

At the foot of the stairs to the left, behind lamp post #0005, is a London plane, *Platanus* x *acerifolia*. (The "x" in a scientific name indicates that the plant is a hybrid, not a true species.) The common name derives from the tree's proven ability to survive city hardships in London. It is so firmly established as a streetside tree that it is a bit out of place in a naturalistic park whose stated purpose, in Olmsted's words, is "that of relieving the visitor from the city."

The London plane is a hybrid between the American sycamore, *P. occidentalis,* and a Eurasian species, *P. orientalis.* The hybrid carries as many as four fruit balls

3

in a cluster and shows bright yellow underbark when it peels, whereas the American sycamore has nearly white underbark and bears its fruit singly. The American sycamore is intolerant of city conditions and in addition is subject to anthracnose, a fungus disease that defoliates and weakens the trees even in favorable sites. It is doubtful whether any American sycamore survives in the city so you can be sure that any so-called sycamore is really a London plane.

Directly uphill from the London plane is another Osage orange, larger than the first. Its two trunks have each produced a branch that crosses the other and has merged with it as a natural graft in the shape of a capital D.

At the foot of the steps, take the left fork of the path. The first tree near the path, about 10 feet ahead on the right, is a sycamore maple, *Acer pseudo-platanus,* with another farther ahead on the left. This is one of the most easily distinguished maples so take a moment to memorize the characteristics. The bark is rough and, on mature trunks, peels in irregular flakes. Leaves are dark green and heavy textured, with conspicuously raised veins on the underside. Leafstalks are often red. The greenish yellow flowers, borne in long grapelike clusters, appear in May after the leaves have developed. The fruits, called keys, also in long chains, are bent downwards at a sharp angle, sometimes with their wings nearly parallel. The fruit clusters remain on the tree until after the leaves have fallen, affording an instant means of identification. This European introduction, like the English sparrow, is invasive. Its rampant seedlings often choke out slower growing, more desirable trees.

Just before you reach lamp post #0007, in line with a rock on the right of the path, is a pin oak, *Quercus palustris,* too young to demonstrate the drooping lower branches that characterize mature specimens but with

4

leaves low enough to examine. Pin oaks belong to the red oak section, with sharply pointed, needle-tipped lobes. Pin oak leaves are the smallest in the pin-red-scarlet-black group, and are shiny, deeply cut, and smooth underneath except for tufts of rusty-tan down in the axils of the veins. Buds are brown and hairless. The bark pattern isn't much help in identification, being a rather haphazard mixture of light gray patches and broken areas of near black. However, here's a layman's crutch: the lobes of the leaves tend to be cruciform, that is, standing out at right angles from the main axis of the leaf. In contrast, the lobes of the other oaks in the group point forward towards the tip of the leaf. More than anything, the airiness of the canopy—even on enormous specimens such as we shall see later on this walk beyond the Glen Span—is the easiest mark of recognition. After you have become familiar with the pin oak's lacy pattern and dappled shade, you will be confident that you can identify at least one oak at first glance.

Halfway between lamp post #0007 and the next lamp post on the left, about 25 feet up the slope, stands a tulip tree, *Liriodendron tulipifera.* This is one of our most regal natives, reaching 200 feet under optimum conditions, with a trunk often clear of branches for 80 feet or more. Walk along to the next lamp post where another tulip tree, even taller than the first, hangs a low branch over the path. Here you can examine the leaves and, if it is early June of a favorable year, admire the large tuliplike flowers of light green and orange. Because the tree is so tall and the flowers borne so high, many people never notice them, but the sharp-eyed Linnaeus who named the tree celebrated its flowers twice over in botanical Greek and Latin: lily-tree tulip-bearer.

With the tulip tree we are on solid ground. No other tree has its exclusive leaf pattern: squared off and with a broad wedge cut out of its tip. This is a reassuring

5

certainty to recognize instantly whenever you see it. Even in winter it has a positive identification factor: tan cone-like fruits stand out conspicuously against the sky. Even after the winged seeds are shed, the spikes that bore them remain upright on the branch tips.

Near the edge of the Pool on your right is a Salamon's willow, *Salix* x *sepulcralis*. It is a hybrid between the white and weeping willows and stands midway between them in habit, with semi-erect branches and drooping shoots.

To the willow's left is a pinnate leafed tree, *Ailanthus altissima,* the Tree-of-Heaven that grows in Brooklyn. Its grandiose name indicates no celestial beauty but refers to the rate at which this rampant weed reaches for the sky. A less flattering name, Stink Tree, accurately describes the smell of flowers of the male tree and of the crushed foliage. This is a female tree so you needn't hold your nose in flowering time.

The ailanthus is a comforting certainty in the realm of compound leafed trees. You can identify it with your eyes closed. Run the lobes at the base of the leaflet between your fingers and you will read in Braille the ailanthus's exclusive signature: hard round glands smaller than a pinhead. If you can't reach a leaf, look for the thumblike basal lobes that distinguish the ailanthus from other trees with slender pinnate leaflets: walnut, ash, hickory, cork tree, and sumach. Flowers are inconspicuous but in midsummer female ailanthus trees are crowned with huge cascading clusters of winged fruits. Bright red in the best form, these fruits are easily mistaken for flowers and give the tree a fantastically tropical air.

Beyond the ailanthus, still on the shore of the Pool, is a bald cypress, *Taxodium distichum,* a tree native to our southern swamps but hardy as far north as New England. In its native range, the soaring column of the trunk can top 140 feet and is in effect the Easterner's giant sequoia. The bark, finely grooved and cinnamon colored, is smooth except for fibrous shreds. The pale green, feathery needles turn bright amber before dropping in autumn, leaving the tree naked or bald, a trait it shares with only a few conifers: the larches, golden larch, and metasequoia.

Turning again to the left, a few feet above the path, just before the unnumbered lamp post, you will see two maples. The rear one has horizontal keys like those of the Norway maple but all other details of bark, leaf, and dangling clusters of fruit agree with those of the sycamore maple. The seedlings around these trees show the red leafstalks which are a good but not unfailing clue to identity. The number of volunteers explains why this coarse and invasive tree is entirely too prevalent in Central Park.

Beyond the lamp post, up the slope and almost against the wall, are three more sycamore maples, the last or most northerly having conspicuous red key fruits. This is the variety *A. p. erythrocarpum*—almost decorative enough to redeem this dull and overused species.

Turn to the shoreline before you walk farther. The small gray-barked tree leaning to the south is a hackberry, *Celtis occidentalis.* Hackberries are one of the most prolifically self-sown trees in Central Park. If you learn to recognize them, you'll be well on your way to knowing the park's trees. Perversely, the hackberry grows best in austere rock crevices and mopes when furnished with open soil and ample moisture. This sickly specimen, suffering from wet feet, is introduced for identification only.

The hackberry's witches' brooms, a proliferation of twiggy growths caused by a mite-borne fungus, are an easy means of recognition when they are present. If you depend on brooms alone, you'll never recognize the immune strain of hackberry, so let's have a careful look at the more stable characteristics. The leaves are light green and fresh looking, with a long tapering tip as if the end of the leaf had been pinched and drawn out between the fingers. The leaf base is asymmetrical, as befits a member of the elm family, and smooth margined; the terminal edges are toothed. The fruit, a small round berry borne on a scant half inch stalk in the leaf axils, is a valuable food for wild birds. Bark is extremely variable and may be as smooth as a beech bole or broken into warts and corky ridges.

On the left as you walk ahead are three sycamore maples in a straight line. Beyond them is a European hornbeam, *Carpinus betulus*, with two slender trunks. The fruit clusters of the European hornbeam are made up of bracts 1½ inches long, with rounded tips like the end of a finger, and usually not toothed on the margin. By comparison, the bract of the American hornbeam is much smaller, usually less than ¾ inch long, and is a pointed triangle with one or more teeth on the edge. If fruit is absent (and the American hornbeam is very sparse in fruiting) identification rests on the winter buds: ¼ inch in the European, ⅙ inch or less in the American. In general the European hornbeam is a fairly substantial tree with a dense canopy, while the American is slight, open, and delicate in appearance. These are admittedly very tenuous clues, and explain why every non-fruiting hornbeam has had its identification shifted back and forth many times and sometimes left unresolved.

Turn right at lamp post #0105. The sycamore maple on the right is old enough to show the mature bark pattern of irregular, roughly circular flakes. Ahead is a thoroughly dull stretch where commonplace street trees, easily obtained but barren of interest, have been used to replace the original varied planting. Let's leave the path and walk down towards the Pool. The tree at the water's edge is a pin oak, this time mature enough to show the drooping lower branches that give it a highly individual silhouette, easily recognized even in winter. Note again the small, deeply cut leaves with lobes at right angles to the main axis, and the airy effect of the canopy when seen against the sky.

As you look across the Pool to the far bank, you can see two pipes or culverts, the ignominious housing of Montanye's Rivulet, one of the few natural streams still visible in Manhattan. It takes its name from Abraham de la Montanye who owned land extending to the north and east. Montanye sold the eastern portion to one Nutter whose name survives in Nutter's Battery on the highlands overlooking Harlem Meer. This was one of a series of fortifications along the northern cliffs, dating from the War of 1812 and including the still extant Blockhouse, the oldest building in Central Park.

The brook called Montanye's Rivulet flowed northeast between two ridges and emptied into Harlem Creek. It is the only natural brook that Olmsted retained in Central Park. "Mere rivulets are uninteresting," he wrote, "and we have preferred to collect the ornamental water in large sheets, and to carry off through underground drains the water which at present runs through the park in shallow brooks." For this purpose, he dammed the brook to create the Pool and Cascade and, beyond the Glen Span, widened it to form the Loch.

Olmsted evidently felt that the newly formed Pool demanded a grander source than modest little Montanye's Rivulet. Somewhat to the left on the far side, largely screened by bushes from this viewpoint, a more dramatic spring gushes from a man-made cavern and falls over a rocky ledge, as we shall see later at close hand.

A fair-sized tree stands alone on the far bank between the natural spring and the artificial one. This is a sour gum, *Nyssa sylvatica*, also called tupelo and pepperidge.

9

You can see the high gloss of the leaves and—often as early as August—a flickering of red. This tree is the first to show a change to autumn color, and ends in a spectacular display of scarlet or mahogany red. It is regrettable that this splendid native resents root disturbance and is almost impossible to transplant. The best way to produce a colony—far more effective than an isolated specimen—is to stop mowing the grass and hope for seedlings or suckers from the roots.

The branch pattern of the sour gum is so distinctive that you can recognize it at a distance. The trunk usually rises like a mast, not dividing, but producing many short, roughly horizontal branches throughout its length. With age, the leader often dies and a side branch takes its place, growing up at an angle to give the tree a wonderfully picturesque, windswept look.

Coming back to the bank we stand on and walking to the east, we pass beneath a London plane and find a new tree, a red or swamp maple, *Acer rubrum*. This maple justifies its name in four seasons: red flowers on naked twigs in earliest spring, red key fruits, glorious yellow-orange-red autumn color, and red winter buds. The leaves are small, thin textured, mostly three lobed, and with a grayish cast underneath. The bark is smooth and light gray on young trunks and upper branches, and dark gray and broken on mature trees. The wide-ranging surface roots are characteristic of trees that grow by choice in wet places. At one time the trunk of this specimen divided in two, then reconsidered and grew back together again in a natural graft.

Let's return to the footpath now. At the point where it branches off sharply to the northwest, about 8 feet from a lamp post, is a tree with pinnately compound leaves— not an ailanthus, as you can tell by the absence of basal lobes.

When you start to identify an unknown tree, look first

at the branch pattern. In the great majority of trees, the twigs are alternate, that is, arranged in a staggered row along the branch. Among native trees, only three have opposite, or paired, twigs: maple, ash, and dogwood, usually rendered as MAD as an aid to memory. This code word was designed for field work; in the parks we meet exotic trees as well as natives. To include paulownia and phellodendron (under a single P) and horsechestnut, I have scrambled the letters to read DAMPh. (The reason for the small *h* is found on p. 47 but I suggest you wait until you come to it rather than clutter your mind with exceptions before you have mastered the primary rules.)

The opposite-branched trees can then be sorted out according to leaf type, as follows:

Dogwood: simple leaves
Ash: pinnate leaves
Maple: simple leaves
Paulownia: simple leaves
Phellodendron: pinnate leaves
Horsechestnut: palmate leaves.

Put a marker in the page so you can return to it readily, and now have an analytical look at the tree in question. It has opposite branches and pinnate leaves: it could be either ash or phellodendron (cork tree). In the ash, the winter bud is visible in the axil of the main leafstalk where it joins the twig. In the cork tree, the base of the leafstalk is conical: it entirely encloses and conceals the bud in its hollow end.

Since the bud is visible, this is an ash. Turn a leaflet over: it is pale green, not white, and is set directly on the main stalk without a stalk of its own. This is the mark of the green ash, *Fraxinus pennsylvanica* var. *subintegerrima*. If you can find a fallen branch, you can clinch the identification by studying the leaf scar with a hand lens. The green ash has semicircular scars, almost flat across the top except for a slight indentation for the bud. In contrast, the scar of the white ash is crescent shaped. Notice also the irregular bark pattern of broken V's and chevrons, distinct from the white ash's continuous ridges.

Across the path is a magnificently sculptured rock with an English holly, *Ilex aquifolium,* set in front of it. This is a handsome plant with glossy, wavy-edged leaves and green stems, far superior in decorative effect to the dull-leafed American holly, but out of harmony with this wild setting. Its habit is too stiff and formal to relate to the flowing contours of the rock with which it competes for attention. It would be far better to tie the exposed ends of the rock to the earth with a planting of fountainy shrubs, and to keep any foreground planting low and inconspicuous.

The high ground beyond the rock is Bogardus Hill, site of Bogardus House where Olmsted lived with his family while he was laying out Central Park. It was Olmsted's practice to survey the grounds on horseback, keeping a sharp eye on progress and always alert to make changes in contour when a new rock outcrop was uncovered. I like to think that Olmsted rode out into the park through this quiet valley, and that it received his first and last thoughts of the working day.

Black cherries, *Prunus serotina,* cluster around the lamp post at the left. The leaves are shining and acrid-smelling when crushed. The underside is marked by conspicuous brushes of reddish brown hair along the midrib near the base. White flowers are carried in fingerlike racemes and ripen to sprays of glossy black cherries, pleasantly bitter to the taste, invaluable food for wild birds, and exceedingly useful to moisten the mouth if all the drinking fountains you pass are out of order.

On the opposite side of the path is a fairly large compound leafed tree, a new one for this walk. Let's tackle it by elimination. It has no basal glands so it isn't an

12

ailanthus. Its branches are alternate so it isn't an ash. The three terminal leaflets are larger than the basal ones, and this points to a hickory. The terminal buds aren't yellow so this isn't a bitternut; the bark isn't shaggy so it isn't a shagbark. The only other hickory that commonly has five leaflets is the pignut, *Carya glabra*, and that's what we have here. Look for nuts in their pear-shaped husks on the branches, or perhaps you'll find one on the ground, discarded by a squirrel as too tough to bite through. If you find one, note the final clue to identity: the husk is grooved to split only about halfway to the base.

Just beyond the hickory are two more black cherries, then a neat, low branched tree on a rocky point. This is a variety of the oriental white mulberry, *Morus alba* var. *tatarica*, with smaller leaves and more regular habit than the sprawly type, and also much hardier. Note the orange tinge in the bark and on exposed roots, a mark of kinship with the Osage orange which belongs to the mulberry family. Mulberry leaves are variable in the number of lobes they show. Those with five to seven lobes suggest miniature fig leaves, and properly so, as figs also belong to the mulberry family. Ripe mulberries are sweetish and rather insipid to human taste but are enthusiastically gobbled by birds.

Now turn and look uphill. At the near end of the first bench stands one of our most magnificent native trees, the sweet gum, *Liquidambar styraciflua*. Its wide-spreading surface roots, like those of the red maple, indicate a liking for moist places. Sit in its shade to admire the clean-cut star shape of its leaves against the sky. This is one of the welcome trees that you can master at once and recognize instantly on next encounter. Spiny fruit balls clinch the identification. Look for them on the ground or dangling from the branches—little green burs at first, then turning brown and woody as they ripen.

The special glory of the sweet gum is in its autumn

13

color which includes not only yellow and apricot tones but also the rarer rose-reds and bronzy purples. As trees tend to color more vividly when growing close to water, this tree is one to seek out when leaves turn in October.

If this is one of the blessed days when cars are banned and the park is a haven of tranquility as Olmsted intended, you can enjoy the song of birds with bullfrog obbligato. As you look across the sheet of water to the reflected willows and woods beyond, you can imagine yourself truly transported to the country. Olmsted wrote, "Every bit of work done on the Park should be done for the single purpose of making the visitor feel as if he had got far away from the town." It is a measure of the designers' genius that this illusion is created within a hundred yards of the bustling city.

If you're refreshed and ready to tackle a new tree, look at the little-leaf linden, *Tilia cordata*, standing between the far end of the bench and the next lamp post. There is no essential difference between the little-leaf and European linden except in leaf size: the former from 1½ to 3 inches long, the latter 2½ to 4 inches. Admittedly there's a bit of overlapping in the middle, but you'll be doing quite well enough if you recognize a linden. The boat-shaped bract which bears buds, flowers, and then seeds on its lower surface is common to all lindens and is a valuable clue to identity. When seeds are ripe, the dry bract acts as a sail to spin the seeds away on the wind, far from the shadow of the parent tree.

The bracts and flowers are used in Europe to make an herbal tea, recommended for a wide range of ailments from insomnia to flatulence. I hope the medicinal properties of the tea are more substantial than its flavor: prolonged boiling produced only a faint taste of straw. The value of European lindens is more solidly based on their beautifully symmetrical form and the sultry, pervasive fragrance of their flowers. Honey derived from

14

linden blossoms preserves their heady perfume, the essence of sunny June, for the winter breakfast table.

Twenty feet up the slope behind the lamp post on the left is a large white ash, *Fraxinus americana,* which you recognize first by its opposite branching and pinnate leaves. The underside of the leaflet is whitish, with fine white hairs along the central vein and in varying degrees in the vein axils. Leaflets are attached to the main leaf-stalks by individual stalks of their own. On mature white ashes, the bark pattern is of linked diamonds in continuous ridges, not the broken pattern of the green ash.

Ashes, like ailanthus, hollies, cork trees, Osage oranges, and ginkgos, are separately sexed—that is, a male tree produces only staminate or pollen-bearing flowers, while another tree bears female flowers which, when pollinated, develop into fruit. You might take this tree for a female because it appears to bear clusters of black fruit. It is in fact a male. The berrylike objects are flowers blackened by a fungus disease that affects some male white ashes.

Move along to the next row of benches. Behind the first one, 40 feet up the slope, is a female white ash, loaded in summer with clusters of slender paddle-shaped fruit. In winter when the seeds have been shed, you may still be able to see the stiff strings on which they grew. If you can reach a low branch, notice the widespread leaf scar, as individual as a fingerprint.

To a sportsman, the white ash is the king of trees. Its wood is nearly as strong as hickory but much lighter in weight. It is pliable, easily worked and bent into shape, and resistant to splitting and splintering. These qualities make white ash the first choice for the frames of small boats and tennis rackets, for the floors of bowling alleys, and to make oars, paddles, hockey sticks, and baseball bats.

Behind the white ash, just a little to its right, is a smaller tree, a bitternut hickory, *Carya cordiformis,* the

15

one with the unmistakable bright yellow buds. If the grass isn't too wet, walk in to fix this key in your mind. Fruits, if you can find one, have ridges or wings along the outer end of the husk. Here is a good opportunity to compare the leaf pattern of ashes and hickories: the leaflets of the ash mostly uniform in size, while the three outer leaflets of the hickory are markedly larger than the basal ones. Note too the great beauty of the bark of this young hickory: pinkish tan in the crevices, pale gray on the shallow, rounded ridges. The bark of mature hickories becomes greatly roughened so this is merely an added enjoyment, not a reliable mark of identity.

As you turn back to the path, you will have no difficulty in naming the big tree with its trunk pressed against a rock. The indented end of the leaf infallibly spells tulip tree.

On the point of land that juts out into the Pool is a well placed swamp or red maple. This tree is indicated in Louis Harmon Peet's *Trees and Shrubs of Central Park*, published in 1903, approximately thirty years after landscaping of the park was completed, and therefore a fairly accurate record of the original plant material.

Maples are not long lived trees. The dead crown and limbs of this specimen reflect its age and also injury to the surface roots from erosion and trampling. A replacement should be planted nearby so that it will have reached considerable size by the time the old tree succumbs.

Within the triangle where paths fork ahead, there is a double-flowering English hawthorn, *Crataegus oxycantha*, a garden subject somewhat out of place in a natural setting. Fortunately it is being shaded to death by the overhanging London plane. A silverbell, *Halesia carolina*, with a thicket of redbud, *Cercis canadensis*, at its feet, would be an agreeable replacement, well suited to the woodland ecology.

To underline the wisdom of using wild plants in wild

16

places, look up into the woods to the left where trees and rocks form an unstudied composition. All that is needed are some saplings and understory trees—perhaps the silverbell's lovely cousin, *Styrax japonica,* or shrubby dogwoods—and a few spreading shrubs and ferns to help close the gaps between the tree trunks. When the leafy canopy is dense enough, the intruding grass will be shaded out, and the woodland atmosphere will then be as authentic as Olmsted left it.

Walk along the grassy triangle, stop on the point nearest the bridge, then walk about 40 feet into the woods. Behind a mass of privet, an inexcusably banal plant whose elimination should stand high on the priority list of improvements in Central Park, is a large bitternut hickory, easily known by its bright yellow buds. Unlike the young tree we saw earlier, this one shows the rough bark of mature trees.

Midway between the hickory and the road, on the edge of the cliff overlooking the stream, there is a large tree with low, horizontal, opposite branches. Even if you can't reach a leaf, you can tell by the stalked leaflets and continuously ridged bark that this is a white ash. Young saplings are valuable because their leaves are within reach, but it is advisable to study the overall picture of mature trees as well.

Return to the path and pass under some black locusts near the bridge. You will recall their thin-textured, oval, pinnate leaflets and the deeply grooved bark. At the far end of the bridge, on the left, is another compound leafed tree. Try it yourself now: alternate branches, large terminal leaves, bright yellow buds. Did you come up with a bitternut hickory? This one shows the rough bark of a mature tree at the base and the delicately colored juvenile bark at eye level. As this tree branches low, take the opportunity to examine the buds with your hand lens. The bud is long and covered with two scales whose edges

17

meet without overlapping. When you add a dusting of yellow-gold powder, you have a dependable key to fix in memory.

Circle around the end of the Pool, turn left at lamp post #0227, and walk down the steps to view the Cascade from below. Note how the scene has changed in just a few steps from the serene expanse of the Pool to a rocky gorge. Look back to the two giant trees flanking the steps. Both are in critical condition, possibly as a result of having their roots smothered in asphalt. The tree on the right is a venerable tulip tree, shown in Peet; on the left, a red oak so far gone in decay that it is an acute danger to walkers on this path. A huge wound on the trunk, not protected by tree dressing, is now rotted and riddled by carpenter ants. The tree should be taken down at once, with deep regret for the loss of a forest giant for lack of elementary care.

The boulders scattered over the banks of the gorge were not meant to be exposed but to serve as soil retainers and supports for luxuriant planting. Olmsted, who aimed at giving park visitors as wide a variety of landscape experiences as possible, wrote out clear directions for "the tranquil, open, pastoral scenes" which were to predominate in the park, and "landscape passages *strongly contrasting.* . . . in complexity of grouping, and the frequent density, obscurity, and wild intricacy of low growing foliage, especially on broken and rock-strewn surfaces."

All that survives is a pleasant tangle of wisteria and viburnum high on the far bank, and, in the barren rocks, an infestation of the viciously invasive Japanese knotweed, *Polygonum cuspidatum.* With intelligent selection of suitable plants—clethra, aronia, shadbush, native rhododendrons, and perhaps Virginia creeper and akebia to drape the rocks—this bleak rockpile could be turned into a scene of luxuriant beauty.

The arch of Glen Span is repeated against the sky by

18

two great trees, a hybrid elm on the left whose branches meet those of a European beech on the right—a superb piece of planting on a grand scale to match the Span. The tasteless thicket of privet below the beech, and a clumsy attempt to check erosion with a dike of small stones, emphasize the need of a highly qualified landscape architect to direct all planting and construction in the park. If this slope were secured by a billowing mass of shrubs and tangled vines, cribbing would not be necessary and the big trees, now isolated, would rise out of a bank of greenery.

The arch frames an enticing picture, if you can overlook the rubbish and beer cans or if you follow a clean-up by the Litter Brigade of the Friends of Central Park. Each underpass was designed, like the curtain in a theater, to make a transition between scenes of varying mood. Here the water, leaving the rugged cascade, opens into a meandering brook, alive with birds which feed in the shrubbery and stop to drink and bathe in the shallow riffles. Stroll beside the stream as you savor one of the unspoiled delights of Central Park: the city entirely screened from view, and no sounds but bird song and the music of water rippling over stones.

Follow the trail until you come to a crosswalk at lamp post #0239. Just ahead on the left are an extraordinary pair of two-trunked red oaks, *Quercus rubra*. Look first at the bark pattern: broad stripes of smooth pale gray on a dark and broken background. Leaves are larger and broader than those of pin oaks, dark green and dull-surfaced above, lighter green below, and hairless except for axillary tufts. The leafstalks are often tinged with red. The buds are the final check: shining red or red-brown and without hairs except for an occasional sparse fringe at the tips of the bud scales.

All the trees in this key woodland area are in critical need of remedial care. Some of them, broken and decayed

19

beyond recall, should be removed and replaced with vigorous youngsters.

The Friends of Central Park can't redeem this forsaken forest but they have made a start. With funds generously contributed by Mr. and Mrs. Jacob Kaplan, the Friends engaged the Bartlett Tree Company to treat these two notable oaks. It took two full working days to secure the diverging trunks with cables, punch holes in the frozen ground to get fertilizer to the feeding roots, and clear the trees of long-dead stubs and broken limbs. It was a great relief to find that the decaying branches had not rotted back to form cavities. The trunks are sound and the investment well justified. Aside from prolonging the life of these outstanding oaks, the work demonstrates that trees can be restored to health and beauty if they are rescued in time.

In contrast to Bartlett's correct pruning and careful wound protection, aimed at promoting rapid healing, notice the mangled willows along the stream. Cuts have been made in total ignorance of the process of growth. One leader has been cut directly across, leaving a stub that can't possibly heal. Not one of the cuts has been sealed with wound dressing.

Central Park's world-famous landscape demands the same level of highly skilled professional care as any art treasure in a museum. It is intolerable that workmen are permitted to use saws without first being taught approved pruning techniques or having a supervisor stand by to train them on the spot.

Olmsted and Vaux were not merely artists but profound humanitarians. Even though the tract set aside for the park was surrounded only by fields and farms, the designers foresaw the time when these open spaces would be solidly built up. It was for the future residents of the growing city that Olmsted and Vaux sought "immunity from the bustling, violent, and wearing influences" of the streets by "the constant suggestion to the imagination of an unlimited range of rural conditions." For a wide variety of experience, tranquil pastoral meadows were contrasted with rugged, picturesque sylvan scenery where, in Olmsted's words, "although the eye never penetrates far, an agreeable suggestion is conveyed to the imagination of freedom, and of interest beyond the objects which at any moment meet the eye."

The wild areas of the Ramble and northern woods do in fact offer a marvelous stimulus to the imagination, an invitation to explore the unseen wilderness over the hill, and have afforded adventure to generations of city-bound children. These forested areas, whether natural or created, are Central Park's unique treasure. In the early days of the last century, beautifully landscaped cemeteries were the city dweller's favorite Sunday promenade until botanic gardens and golf courses took their place. These are welcome open spaces of neatly cultivated lawns and trees, but only in Central Park can you find the essence of wildness.

This stretch of forest will be treasured by naturalists when our city children at last get an Audubon Nature Study Center. Here can be demonstrated the growth of a climax forest, the cycle of the seasons, the action of water, soil management, seed dispersal, and the interdependence of man and animals on tree and plant life. When an enlightened civic leader, at some not far distant time, understands the proper use of urban park land and its inestimable educational value, our children will be given this vital learning experience. The authentic atmosphere of a natural forest can be restored at a very small outlay when compared with the vast sums thrown away on trashy, short-term amusements.

The teardrop-shaped grassy island just ahead contains a mica-glinting rock, lamp post #0243, and a black oak, *Quercus velutina*. When growing in favorable conditions, the black oak is characterized by a majestic spread of massive limbs, horizontal or drooping. Leaves are larger than those of pin and red oak, and may be 12 inches long and more than half as broad. The unthrifty condition of this specimen may be due to the rock-underlaid soil it must root in. Perhaps its sparse, narrow branching may reflect an admixture of pin oak blood. (Oaks are notoriously free hybridizers.) However, all other details agree with black oak specifications: rough black bark breaking into small plates; leaves lustrous dark green above, rusty-pubescent below; twigs and leafstalks downy; buds four-angled, dull dark brown and matted with gray hairs. If you remember that *velutina* means velvety, you will have a memory hook for the black oak.

Walk out to the rock ledge overlooking the stream which broadens into the Loch just beyond. The shrub on the right, with low arching branches and big asymmetrical leaves is a native witchhazel, *Hamamelis virginiana,* a refreshing nonconformist that opens its spidery, straw yellow flowers in November.

There is a senseless cat's cradle of asphalt paths here, wandering in every direction but the needed one, that is, leading straight from Glen Span. Asphalt even obscures part of the rocky overlook. If this needless hard surface were removed and its site planted with low shrubs, the woodland quality would be to a great extent restored, and the trees would benefit from pervious soil over their roots instead of a blanket of asphalt.

If you choose to walk along the Loch to the next cascade and through Huddlestone Bridge, you will see how the landscape has been violated by the Lasker Rink. Nothing that the infamous Tweed Ring inflicted on Olmsted and Vaux's masterpiece can equal the towering vulgarity of this encroachment. Once an outrage is admitted, it spreads its contagion far beyond its actual boundary. Because of faulty design, the basement of the rink is

flooded each spring, with consequent damage to costly electronic equipment. It is now proposed to confine the far end of the Loch in a culvert, thus destroying still more of the natural scenery to reinforce the primary blight.

Let's resume our stroll through the woodland, retracing our steps towards Glen Span. Just before reaching it, look across the brook to the largest tree near the abutment. This is a magnificent pin oak, displaying even in maturity the lacelike effect of its canopy.

After going under Glen Span and up the steps, pick up the path around the south side of the Pool. After you pass the first row of benches and lamp post #0115, look for a low rock outcrop on the left. The next large tree is a new one for this walk, a white oak, *Quercus alba*. This has the rounded lobes and sinuses of the white oak group, in contrast to the sharp, needle-pointed leaves of the red oak section. The white oak is easily recognized by its pale gray bark, peeling off in long flakes that get larger and looser towards the top of the tree. This specimen is young, but in a hundred years or so, it should develop the mature white oak's noble bearing, with a canopy often broader than it is tall.

The white oak holds an honored place in American history: white oak ship timbers supplied a lifesaving cash crop for the first colonists to send back to England in exchange for vital supplies. White oaks are much too scarce in Central Park. Their low, full outline would help to fill the gaps around the border of the Sheep Meadow and East Meadow as the more open and mercilessly limbed-up pin oaks cannot do. The long-lived beauty and historical interest of white oaks should commend them to thoughtful donors.

Walk ahead to the iron rail fence. On your left is the cavern that conceals the man-made spring. It is topped by a tulip tree which you should by now name without hesitation. The whole mound, especially the jumble of

24

rocks that forms the frame of the cave, should be mantled in a jungle of shrubs and vines, with ferns and creepers to veil the harsh line of the lintel. The present skimpy planting does nothing to create the illusion of naturalness.

For a surprise, go down the step on the far side of the falls. Here is a hidden rock seat where you can rest in a secret grove. A film of water has been made to slide over an existing rock, following its crevices and gathering into tiny pools where birds flock to drink and bathe.

When you return to the footpath and continue walking towards Central Park West, you will see a drinking fountain and a smooth-leafed elm, *Ulmus carpinifolia*, with an imposing burled trunk which divides about 5 feet above ground. Elms are exceedingly difficult to distinguish even in pure strains—there is in fact no acknowledged authority nor definitive monograph—and they hybridize as freely as oaks do. *U. carpinifolia* has rather small leaves, 2 to 4 inches long, smooth on both sides except for downy tufts in the vein axils. This species and the English elm, *U. procera,* are indistinguishable at a distance, as both have short, stout trunks with or without suckers sprouting from trunk and roots. The English elm, however, has notably rough leaves: the upper surface is covered with minute stiff hairs, visible under a hand lens and feeling like sandpaper when a finger is drawn across the leaf.

The root suckers of this specimen have been trampled to death near the base of the tree but a little colony has established itself farther up the bank. The low-dipping branches of a nearby European hornbeam touch the elm suckers and give you a second chance to look for the intricately designed fruit clusters dangling from the tree or, in late summer, covering the ground. Squirrels sometimes bite off the clusters to get at the tiny nutlet in the cupped base of the bracts, thus providing a specimen which you may collect for further study without charge of vandalism.

As you walk towards the street, look up the hill to the left, at the edge of the road, to admire an ancient and majestic horsechestnut which divides into five main trunks. This tree is charted in Peet and may be considered part of the original planting of Central Park. Its giant branches, each as thick as a normal tree, arch over road and path to make a fitting climax for our first walk in the magic countryside created by Olmsted and Vaux in the heart of the city.

> "It is one great purpose of the Park to supply to the hundreds and thousands of tired workers, who have no opportunity to spend their summers in the country, a specimen of God's handiwork that shall be to them, inexpensively, what a month or two in the White Mountains or the Adirondacks is, at great cost, to those in easier circumstances."
>
> *Frederick Law Olmsted*

II

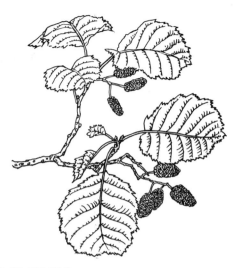

CONSERVATORY
WATER

72nd Street and
Fifth Avenue

I N this mid-length tour you will meet some exciting new
oaks and refresh your acquaintance with more familiar
sorts. In addition there are two uncommon trees, a European alder and an Oriental beech, not seen on any other
tour, plus a highly controversial ash whose precise identity
is still in dispute.

An ideal time to start this walk is about an hour before
sunset. As you reach its end by twilight, you will see
Conservatory Water in its most spellbinding guise, remote
and softly luminous in the afterglow.

The section covered on this tour is notable for the large number of trees surviving from the original planting, a concentration found nowhere else in the park. These venerable trees lend a long-established air to the scene. Their quality testifies to the taste and creative imagination of the designers.

Olmsted literally searched the world for rare trees to grace Central Park. The formal area centering on the Mall, envisioned as a commanding element in the design, was one of the first to be developed. As Olmsted wrote, "If I recollect rightly, in 1859 the trees (were planted) about the Mall and east of it, and on both sides the 72nd Street entrance road . . ." It is likely that the choicest specimens in the nursery were given prominent place in this key section.

The first and perhaps most remarkable of these treasures stands near the Fifth Avenue entrance. As you face the park, take the path to the left of the road. Pass the traffic light on your right and continue about 100 feet to an enormous tree behind benches on your left. Its trunk is enclosed in a scrap of wire fencing. This is a Chinese elm, *Ulmus parvifolia*, reputed to be the largest of its species in the entire country.

The Chinese elm is a widely variable tree but it is consistent in having thumbnail-sized leaves and a singular habit of flowering in September. A bark pattern of small peeling flakes is typical, most commonly in mottled shades of gray, so the reddish tint of this specimen is unusual. A sturdy nonconformist, the Chinese elm remains green until late in November. In compensation, it is exceedingly cautious about starting growth in spring, and stands bare and apparently dead when other trees are in full leaf. Don't panic! If you examine the swelling buds and feel the supple spring of the twigs, you'll be assured that the tree is indeed alive and just taking its time about stirring from sleep.

28

Conservatory Water

The Chinese elm is resistant to Dutch elm disease and is sometimes advertised as a substitute for the American elm, now wholly wiped out in Central Park. However, the Chinese elm often develops an irregular head—far off balance in this instance—and bears no resemblance to the magnificent fountain-shaped crown of the American elm.

As you walk around the Chinese elm, notice how the diverging trunks have been secured with rods and cables to prevent splitting. You will have to look hard to see the fillings, tinted to match the bark and so expertly installed that new growth has nearly closed over them. This highly skilled work was performed in the pre-Moses days when care of the park landscape was the Park Department's most compelling responsibility and when cherished trees were kept in peak condition by trained arboriculturists.

Early in 1969, the tree was in sorry shape. The branch that overhangs the benches had a bowl-shaped cavity that held water and would in time lead decay back into the heartwood. Smaller cavities had started in the exposed wood of cuts on the trunk. The leader that is linked by cable to a London plane had a rotting stub and a split, nearly dead, hollow branch.

The Friends of Central Park, in their initial program of providing professional care for the park's threatened trees, chose this historic elm as their first candidate for rescue in 1969. The tree was cleared of dead wood and given deep root feeding. The cavity over the benches and the smaller ones in the trunk were chiseled back to sound wood and filled.

When the two failing branches were cut off, it was found that decay had worked back and hollowed the whole leader. In order to clean out and fill the cavity, it would have been necessary to open the entire length of the remaining shell. This would have weakened the column more than filling would benefit it. Instead, the holes were plugged to keep out moisture and thus retard

29

decay. While the effects of long neglect can't be reversed, this treatment, with the help of the supporting cables already in place, will do everything possible to prolong the life of this major leader.

The Friends' effort to preserve the ancient tree is matched by an equally significant gift, a young Chinese elm set at the edge of the lawn to the south. This is a splendid example of conservation and foresighted forestry, by which the life of an aging tree is extended by skilled care, and a young tree is planted nearby to grow on for eventual replacement. Paired gifts of this sort—restoration of a venerable tree and planting a young one of the same species—carry great emotional appeal: a bow to the past in memory of one's parents, and a forward-looking pledge to keep the park green and beautiful for one's grandchildren. These two elms provide an instructive example of enlightened philanthropy. It could well be repeated throughout the park wherever great trees are endangered by lack of essential care.

For an optional tour to see the European alder, continue past the little elm and follow the path as it curves left and then right. You may say with reason that there is little use in studying a tree you won't see again on these tours, but I think it is important to emphasize the unlimited richness of available plant material and the inexcusable banality of recent plantings such as the monotonous stretch of London planes and pin oaks to your right.

As you come out on the main path, turn left and walk past a pin oak behind the benches on your left. The next tree on the left, about 8 feet in back of a bench, is the alder, *Alnus glutinosa,* commonly called tree or black alder. Alders are widely planted in northern Europe because of their extreme hardiness but are largely overlooked in this country. The alder's lengthening male catkins are among the first signs of spring. Some are highly colored: the Manchurian alder, *A. hirsuta sibirica,* has four-inch

30

tassels of warm red-brown, a welcome display above January and February snows. Alders like moist sites and would make ideal plants for bare shores and streamsides such as the Gill in the Ramble.

The black alder has many varieties, some with decoratively cut leaves. This specimen has the standard broad leaves somewhat indented at the tip, like a round canape with one small bite taken out. The underside of the leaf is marked by conspicuously raised veins with tufts of pinkish hairs in the axils. The conelike fruits are the alder's exceptional and enduring beauty. If you stand on the bench to get a close look, you can discover both last year's brown-black cones and this year's green ones and, in autumn, male catkins ready for spring. When you look at a ripened cone through your hand lens, you can appreciate the orderly placement of the scales, arranged in precise spirals which rotate to left and right.

Whether or not you took the alder detour, start again at the traffic light near the ancient Chinese elm and cross the road to the north side. The multiple-stemmed tall shrubs behind the benches to your right are *Cornus mas,* a Eurasian dogwood with mustard-yellow flowers, tiny but profuse, on naked branches in early April. The fruit— clear red, juicy, in size and shape like a small olive—has given the shrub its misleading common name of cornelian cherry. If you recall the code word DAMPh, explained on page 11, you will recognize a dogwood's opposite branching and dismiss the allusion to a cherry.

Look down the path towards the formal pool, called Conservatory Water for a conservatory that was planned for its east side but never built. You are seeing, perhaps without being aware of it, one of Olmsted's devices for "relieving the visitor from the city." As the footpath descends, the trees on the boundary ridge gain in relative height, forming an effective screen. We'll come to the pool by another route, but first let's study the trees on the path that follows the edge of the road.

Beyond the tall lamp post #E 7202, the first tree to the right behind the benches is one that by now you should name with assurance. Its small, sharp-pointed leaves, open canopy, and drooping lower branches all point to the pin oak, *Quercus palustris*. The common name doesn't refer to dressmaker's pins but to the wooden pins or dowels used to frame ships, barns, and houses in the early days of the Colonies when iron nails were scarce and expensive.

Next on the right is a Norway maple, *Acer platanoides*, with others beyond on both sides of the walk. In comparison with the sycamore maple which you will remember from the first tour around the Pool, the Norway maple has tight-fitting bark with an interlacing pattern of shallow ridges. Leaves are thin textured and without prominent veins. Chartreuse flowers in rounded heads are borne on leafless branches in late March or early April, and are followed by key fruits whose horizontal wings resemble an aviator's insignia.

Up ahead on the right, the Pilgrim Father, who didn't land in Central Park, is surrounded by an equally alien scattering of Japanese cherries and giant trumpet daffodils. Olmsted, with his extraordinary taste and foresight, warned against an influx of statues because they broke the sweep of the landscape and invited petty groupings. He wrote:

> "The essence of the park must be in its landscapes. If, as years elapse, the pictorial effects prove to be as broad, well-marked, and varied as was possible under the circumstances of the site, a corresponding measure of success is assured. If, on the other hand, a general impression is conveyed to the eye of a series of groups with comparatively small features, and crowded with details and accessories, the result will

be a failure, however beautiful the details and acces-
sories in themselves may be."

This statue has little to commend it except as an example
of how not to handle a gun: the Pilgrim Father is about
to have his right hand blown off.

It may seem churlish to fault donors who believe they
are adding beauty to Central Park by giving plant material
without the guidance of a historically-trained landscape
architect. Olmsted pointed out the hazard of applying
home garden standards to the profession of park landscaping: "Gardeners and others are apt to think that work
which would be regarded as excellent in a pleasure garden
connected with a private house, or in a fine flower garden,
must be excellent anywhere in Central Park. This is a
great mistake." If you can forget your pleasure in mere
prettiness and consider this grouping in relation to the
surrounding landscape—to the scale of the rugged bluff
across the road to the left, to the rolling hillside that leads
to the ample Conservatory Water—I believe you will see
how meager and irrelevant this addition is.

Another result of putting high-maintenance garden subjects in a park without an adequately trained staff of
gardeners is evident in the last cherry in the group, beyond
the Pilgrim Father and near the path. Its trunk is solidly
white with scale insects which are sucking the life from
this tree and will spread to the others.

Beyond the cherries, still on the right, is a European
weeping birch, *Betula pendula*. This graceful tree is well
situated with plenty of room to display its fountain of
limber branches which lift and sway in every stirring of
air. The birch, like the alder, has conelike fruits but these
are loosely constructed. Their scales, like a string of beads
without a knot, slide off in papery flakes as the seed is
dispersed.

Turn and look back for a moment to see another of

33

Olmsted's tricks for putting the visitor at once in a country setting. Almost as soon as you enter, the path makes a sharp turn and a curtain of trees closes behind you, blotting out the city.

The next tree on the right is a pin oak, planted too close to its neighbor. Olmsted repeatedly, often heatedly, stressed the need for selective thinning after thick planting. On one of his forceful efforts to penetrate the bonehead barrier, he quoted from C. S. Sargent, Professor of Forestry in Harvard University:

> "Thick planting is but following the rule of nature, and thinning is only helping nature do what she does herself too slowly, and therefore too expensively. That is why trees in a plantation intended for ornament, like those in a park or pleasure ground, should be planted thickly at first, and why they should then be systematically thinned from time to time; and it is because this systematic thinning is altogether neglected, or put off until the trees are ruined for any purpose of ornament, that it is so rare to find a really fine tree in any public place or private grounds."

It takes no experience in forest management to realize that when a tree intended as an individual specimen is crowded by an inferior variety, the poorer tree must be removed. By this continual process of selection, weak and straggly trees are eliminated and only the strongest growing and most ornamental remain to grace the park. Refusal to remove a competing tree is represented as reverence for plant life. It is in fact sentimentality of the most destructive sort. Where judicious thinning would produce flourishing, wide-branched specimens, a *laissez faire* policy results in a tangle of misshapen cripples which degrade the quality of the park. Let the late Lord Aberconway, long-time president of the Royal Horticultural Society, have the final word on the rewards of selective thinning. When asked why every single tree on his estate

34

was a magnificent specimen, he replied, "Because I have ruthlessly cut out all the others."

The tree being hollowed by the pin oak is a willow oak, *Quercus phellos*, 8¼ feet in girth. As another survival of the original planting, it deserves preferential care. Its symmetry should be preserved by cutting back intruding branches of less valuable trees.

Just below the crown of the willow oak, a broken stub and a dead branch were encrusted with yellow and orange fungus brackets. Removal of these rotting limbs, a danger to passersby as well as to the tree, was done as part of the Friends' 1969 schedule.

There is always a nerve-wracking moment of suspense when the saw begins to bite, as no one can tell in advance whether decay has entered the trunk through the dead branch and caused a cavity. In this case the outcome was happy: the cut surface was clean and sound.

The willow oak is well named: its leaves are slender and glossy, usually an inch wide or even less. Young leaves have a grayish bloom on the underside and also a decided needle point, but these features tend to disappear as the leaf matures. With your hand lens, examine the network of delicate raised veins on the upper side, as intricate as the pattern of a dragonfly's wing. Acorns are tiny and squat and set in a shallow cup like that of a red oak in miniature.

Come back to the path and continue downhill until you come to a spectacular elm with an extravagantly bewhiskered trunk, at the right of the path opposite a traffic light. This tree is certainly old enough to be part of the original planting and is, I believe, the tree identified by Peet as an English elm. It is in fact a smooth-leafed elm, *Ulmus carpinifolia*, as you can readily tell if you reach a leaf on one of the main branches. Don't be misled by sucker growth on the trunk or roots: leaves on these shoots are

35

seldom typical and in this case feel rough to the touch, while those on branches overhead bear out the name of smooth-leafed elm. If this were an English elm, you could identify it without a hand lens by running a finger over a leaf and feeling the catch of the tiny stiff hairs that stud its upper surface.

The next tree to the right, set a little below the crest of the hill, is an uncommon oak charted by Peet and seen for the first time on our tours. It is a shingle oak, *Q. imbricaria*, named for the ease with which its logs could be rived to form shingles—or, more precisely, shakes, which are split rather than sawed.

The leaves of the shingle oak are unlobed like those of the willow oak but much broader, sometimes over 2 inches wide. The upper surface is a wonderfully rich glossy green, catching and reflecting light, while the underside is paler gray-green. Leaves have slightly rippled margins and are needle tipped, showing kinship with the red oak. Low-dipping branches permit examination of the fringe-like male flowers in spring and of the developing acorns which are on short stalks.

Every detail of this superlative tree is rewarding, and the dramatic pattern of the tortuous branches against the sky makes it one of the park's outstanding treasures. Like the sweet gum, specimens of this handsome, dense headed, clean leafed tree should be used on the borders of meadows or wherever a flimsy plantation needs strengthening.

Next on the right, the four-trunked tree with conspicuously striped bark is a European hornbeam, *Carpinus betulus*. The fruit cluster is made up of three-lobed bracts, each with a nutlet in its cupped base. In the European hornbeam, the central lobe is rounded at the tip and may be 1¾ inches long.

Hornbeams like rich woodland soil, cool and moist. The prolonged drought that started in 1961 killed many hornbeams outright, while others are slowly succumbing to severe root injury. This tree in addition is in an unfavorable site, exposed to a lethal fog of automobile fumes and to compaction of soil through trampling over its roots. It shows the effects of hardship in its small, sparse leaves and many dead twigs. A generous mulch of well-decayed manure or of leafmold might tip the scales on the side of recovery. Hornbeams are invaluable understory trees, just right in scale to provide a transition between shrubs and forest giants. Their chains of fruit are incomparably decorative.

Keep walking downhill and turn right at the intersection. A giant London plane, over 11 feet in girth, stands in the angle of the path. This tree, shown in Peet, is another survivor of the original planting, the stand of ancient trees that gives this area its special distinction. Even though a commonplace variety, the tree's great age and historical significance make it important. For this reason, the cavity on the north side of the trunk was scheduled to be cleaned and filled by the Friends of Central Park in 1969.

In mid-December, when the Bartlett men were working on the Chinese elm, I walked with the foreman to inspect the other trees awaiting treatment. It was only then, after the concealing leaves had fallen, that we discovered that the whole western division of the trunk is hollow. It appears that the leader had died many years before and was not cut away until its decay had penetrated the trunk. If the resulting hole had been plugged, decay might have been arrested or at least retarded. As it is, the trunk is a chimney with squirrels whisking freely in and out at both ends.

Obviously it would do more harm than good to close a cavity near the base when the top is wide open to admit rain. The resources of the Friends had been stretched to cover unexpected filling and repair of the Chinese elm. It was not possible to undertake a major extension of the proposed cavity work on the London plane so this tree was crossed off the Friends' list.

On the left side of the path, across from the London plane, is a small two-trunked tree. This is a fringe tree, *Chionanthus virginicus,* another of the shrubby natives that should be used freely on the edges of clearings in full sun, although you will hardly judge its merits from this puny specimen. In May the flowers are borne in great loose clusters of silky white threads. Male trees have showier flowers but females have the compensation of producing a fine show of fleshy, blue, grape-sized fruit in September. The chionanthus has pale gray bark like a magnolia's, and solid-looking, almost oblong, opposite leaves. Some individuals are treelike in habit while others branch to the ground, making a thicket twenty feet across. If you can visualize some of the thin spots in the planting of the Lake shore, you can imagine how these barren areas would be enriched by the introduction of chionanthus.

Beyond the chionanthus, close to the path, is a very large tree shown in Peet. It defies fitting into any frame of classification. It has caused more perplexity, more return trips for samples, and more arguments than any tree in Central Park.

To start with a certainty, the leaf scars are wide-spreading crescents set back in a series of steps, as is proper with the white ash. The leaflets are thick, almost leathery. Among the numerous varieties of white ash listed in Rehder's *Manual of Cultivated Trees and Shrubs* is *Fraxinus americana* var. *subcoriacea,* described as having thick leaves, silvery white beneath. This doesn't quite fit— varietal descriptions seldom do—as the leaflets of our puzzler have tan undersurfaces. Along the veins, where a typical white ash would have a restrained scattering of white hairs, this specimen has broad bands of gray wool. The stalks of the leaflets are winged on one side nearly to the base, as in red and green ashes. Also, the bark pattern of broken ridges—short V's very like the hoofprints of a deer—is characteristic of red and green ashes and quite unlike the usual white ash's continuously linked diamonds.

Because of the conflicting clues and the unusually thick coating of wool, I was inclined to think that this might be a cross between a white ash and the hairy-leafed red ash. However, there seems to be no record of such a hybrid in botanical literature. While Olmsted was a keen collector of rarities, it is unlikely that he could have chanced on a hybrid that nobody else has observed and described. The clinching factor would be the shape of the winged fruit but I could find none on repeated visits and so assume that the tree is a male.

On the basis of available evidence—chiefly, the crescent leaf scars, the large leathery leaves, and the distribution of hairs—George Kalmbacher sets this down as a highly atypical white ash, perhaps an undescribed variety. As is often the case, research raises more questions than it answers. Anyone with a taste for botanical cryptograms is welcome to join in the fun.

Across the path, a little ahead to the right, a group of three oaks offers an opportunity to review two species and study a new one. The smallest of the three, nearest the path, is a pin oak. It is poorly sited as it interferes both with the visibility and growing room of the other two. To its right as you look uphill is a red oak, *Quercus rubra*, which you saw on the first walk in the woods east of Glen Span. The leaves are larger than those of the pin oak, and are dull surfaced on the underside, with tufts of reddish hair in the vein axils. The bark pattern is not very pronounced on this specimen but the shiny reddish brown buds, hairless except for a slight fringe on the bud scales, are the clinching key to identification. The acorn is large and high domed and is set in a very shallow saucer-shaped cup, just right for serving a grassblade salad or barberry fruit cup at a doll's tea party.

The third oak, to the east of the group, is a scarlet oak, *Q. coccinea*, noted for its blazing autumn color. Its leaves are deeply cut by almost circular sinuses and—the point of recognition—shiny on both sides. Buds resemble those of the red oak but are more brown than red and usually hairy on the outer half. The acorns are comparatively small and are enclosed for more than half their length. The cup is covered by coarse scales but is smooth to the touch, as the scales adhere closely to the surface. This glossy-leafed tree with magnificent fall color deserves wider planting in the park and should be considered as a change from the stiff and over-used pin oak.

Two large black cherries, *Prunus serotina*, make a strong composition as their roots clasp the contours of a rock outcrop farther up the slope. The innate tension in the struggle between an irresistible tree and an immovable rock is charged with drama and should be repeated, with natural variations, wherever such rocks rise above grade.

Across the path is a rare tree which, like the black alder, is the only one of its species encountered on our tours. It stands about 80 feet from the path at the base of a rise and may be singled out by its pale gray bark, much disfigured by carved initials. This is an Oriental beech, *Fagus orientalis*. Like the European beech, its leaf margins are waved but not toothed. The distinguishing mark of the oriental beech is the brush of long silky hairs along the veins underneath and on the leafstalk. The hairs can be seen with the naked eye but you will need a hand lens for the second key: the veins curve inward as they approach the leaf margin.

The planting around the sides and north end of Conservatory Water consists of London planes and pin oaks and is too dull to invite closer inspection. The aesthetic value of the statuary is abysmal even by Central Park standards. Judged as climbing equipment for a playground, it would be rejected as a safety hazard because of the danger of falling on sharp points or onto the hard surface of the base. Let's skip this area which tasteless alterations have left devoid of interest or dignity, and walk to the right around the south end of Conservatory Water.

Up to the early 1930's, before winters grew too warm, this pool was open to the public for ice skating without admission fee. The area is larger than either artificial rink in the park and must have given a marvelous sense of freedom, without wire fence or walls or blare of cheap music to mar the country atmosphere. Skating could have continued on Conservatory Water with a modest endowment for putting down freezing pipes each winter, a true gift of joy to park visitors without any defacement of the beauty of the landscape.

Behind the little brick building—of uncertain utility as it is always tightly shuttered—are three Schwedler maples, *Acer platanoides schwedleri*. This is a red leafed variety of the Norway maple, as the smooth, slightly grooved bark, paper-thin leaves, and horizontal keys attest. The red color is most pronounced in early spring. By midsummer the red tint is largely masked by chlorophyll but the leaves retain an undertone of rich color, an agreeable contrast to the prevailing masses of green.

Go up the steps by an unnumbered lamp post at the southeast corner of Conservatory Water. Across the path and slightly to the right is another red oak, this one showing the red leafstalks that are a welcome if not infallible clue to recognition. This specimen is a compact form with a broad, dense head, a strain selected for street planting where uniformity is desired. The branching habit is heavier and more horizontal than is usual with red oaks but the broad stripes of smooth pale gray on the upper trunk are characteristic.

41

As you walk up the hill, the next tree on your left is a Schwedler maple and beyond it an American linden, *Tilia americana,* with heart-shaped leaves as much as 8 inches long, so large that the tree is sometimes taken for a catalpa at careless glance. However, if you look for the long curved bract which bears buds, flowers, or fruit on its underside, you will quickly recognize the mark of the linden.

American lindens are dying out in Central Park: the hardships of the city environment have passed the limit of tolerance. Trees in the park have two strikes against them at the outset: contaminated air and shallow, impoverished soil. When other harmful factors are piled on —drought, insect infestation, soil compaction, increased summer heat—trees become so weakened that they fall prey to Verticillium Wilt, a fungus disease always present in the soil. In the case of lindens, one damaging agent may be the hordes of aphids that suck juice from the leaves unless controlled by spraying. Perhaps the concentration of air pollutants has reached an intolerable level, as it has with lilacs in the city. Whatever the reasons, it is evident that the American linden will soon go the way of the conifers that once graced Central Park.

Go up the steps, pass the first row of benches, and stop at the unnumbered lamp post. Behind it and to its right are two tall shrubs with rich dark green, pleated leaves. These are *Viburnum sieboldii,* a superb Japanese species which bears large heads of off-white flowers in May and June. The fruit, displayed on widely branching red stems, ripens slowly from pink to red to blue and—unless birds eat it first—ultimately to black. A shrub of this imposing size is better suited to the expanse of park landscape than conventional garden subjects such as forsythia, jetbead, and weigela. Because few home gardens can spare room for *Viburnum sieboldii,* its use in the park combines appropriate scale with a refreshing fillip of novelty.

Directly behind the near end of the solitary bench

farther ahead is a mock orange, one of the innumerable horticultural varieties of *Philadelphus.* This is a useful if not exciting shrub with white flowers—fragrant in the best forms—and a good, low-arching habit. Unfortunately it is extremely attractive to aphids. When unchecked by spraying, they coat the leaves with a sticky exudate which collects soot and makes the plant look grubby.

Fifteen feet behind the far end of the solitary bench is a cut-leaf beech, a variety of the European beech, *Fagus sylvatica.* When wisely planted in full sun and with room to expand, this beech forms a dense mass of horizontal branches, clothed to the ground in a luxuriance of fernlike foliage. This luckless specimen was either planted with no view of its eventual spread, or has been overshadowed by competing trees which should have been removed.

If you're game for a bit of bushwacking, go around behind the bench. About 25 feet behind its center is the rarest oak found on this walk, an English oak, *Quercus robur,* the largest I've found in Central Park. When properly grown, the English oak is a majestic tree with short, thick trunk and wide-spreading, compact head. This tree, like the cut-leaf beech, has become puny through being crowded. Many lower branches are dead: the whole tree is in need of immediate pruning and cutting back of intruding branches of aggressive neighbors.

The living branches are out of reach but the leaf form can be studied on the suckers—not always typical but in this case all that is available. The leaf of the English oak has rounded lobes and sinuses like our native white oak but is much smaller. It has two keys to identification: a leafstalk so short that the leaf seems to sit directly on the twig, and a pair of earlike lobes at the base—auricles, in technical jargon—which arch beside and sometimes overlap the stalk. These auricles are not always evident when leaves first expand but afford an instant mark of recognition in the mature leaf.

Return to the path and walk forward to the Hutchins

43

Memorial. Behind the word TIBI on the back of the bench is a shingle oak, a smaller specimen than the superb one seen earlier, and too crowded ever to achieve the other's perfection of form.

Olmsted, in forming a dense barrier planting to block out the city—"a horizon line composed as much as possible of verdure"—considered trees not as individuals but simply as a screen of mingled foliage. Perhaps cut-leaf beeches and English and shingle oaks were once common enough to be tossed into a mass planting. Under the present impoverished range of park planting, it is regrettable that these choice trees are submerged in a thicket which could be formed as well or better by common trees such as maples.

For a heartening look at the generous effect achieved by discerning park planning, walk to the top of the stairs leading down to the little brick building. Look west to the superb tree that crowns the grassy slope. This is a European linden, *Tilia europea,* whose rounded contour and vast sweeping branches are the perfect complement to Olmsted's ideal of park landscaping, the pastoral meadow: "smooth, simple, clean surfaces of turf on which the light falls early and shadows are broad and trees have grown freely with plenty of room to stretch out their limbs." The springing vigor of the linden is the essence of spaciousness and gives the viewer, as Olmsted intended, "a sense of enlarged freedom."

If you have timed your tour to end at sunset, you will see how the rugged branches of Austrian pines take on new emphasis when silhouetted against the afterglow. As you look down on Conservatory Water in the gathering dusk, the trees on its border draw back into shadow while the sheet of water seems to expand as it mirrors the last gleam of light from the sky.

III

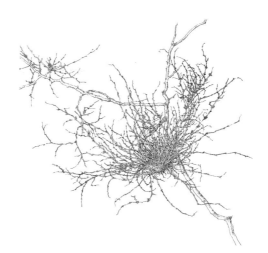

A QUESTION
OF ELMS

93rd Street and
Central Park West

THIS short walk provides an opportunity to study two
unrelated trees with nearly identical bark, to see one of the
park's commonest trees in a form you may not recognize,
and to add a new willow, an English elm, a rare linden,
and a cork tree to the list.

Enter the park just south of 93rd Street and pause inside the gate. On the left, 8 feet from the wall, are two
European willows, *Salix pentandra*. Their common name
of bayleaf willow refers to the dark green, shiny leaves,
finely toothed, hairless, and drawn out into a long point.

The bayleaf willow is easily distinguished from the prevalent white willow and its hybrids by the green, not white, undersurface of its leaves. Its habit tends to be shrubby: even when it assumes tree form, it seldom exceeds a height of 25 feet.

As you walk forward into the park, the next large tree on the left, with its trunk almost touching the path, is a horsechestnut, *Aesculus hippocastanum*. Leaves are palmately compound, that is, radiating from a single point like sticks of a fan. Large panicles of flowers, white tinged with red and gold, stand upright on the branches like candles on a Christmas tree, making a spectacular show in early May. Thick-walled husks contain a single nut with a glossy, bright brown surface, most attractive to sight and touch but reputedly poisonous. The prefix of an animal name—horsechestnut, dogberry, cow parsley—usually has a derogatory meaning, implying that the plant is fit only for beasts. Countrymen used to carry a horsechestnut in their pocket to ward off rheumatism, possibly with the notion that the polished surface of the nut would communicate itself by sympathetic magic to their joints.

Behind the horsechestnut and touching its branches is a large sycamore maple, *Acer pseudo-platanus*, about 4 feet from the playground fence. The bark of both trees shows the same medium gray color and much the same pattern of roughly circular flakes that peel off to show orange-brown underbark.

During the growing season, there is of course no possibility of confusing the compound leafed horsechestnut with the simple leafed maple. In winter when the similar bark invites uncertainty, observe the character of the silhouetted branches. In the maple, the overall impression is of relatively fine twigs and small buds, while the horsechestnut has stout twigs furnished with fat buds, sticky in spring.

Although both maple and horsechestnut start out with

opposite buds, only the maple ends with recognizably opposite branches. The reason is that in the horsechestnut, only one of the paired buds is apt to develop, while the other aborts. Thus it is technically an opposite branched tree even though the majority of its branches are alternate. To point up the paradox, I have indicated the horsechestnut in the code word DAMPh (see page 11) with a small letter, while M stands for maple without qualification.

Walk to the first intersection and pause by the end of the last bench. A small red oak, *Quercus rubra,* stands between two rock outcrops on the right. This is a compact variety selected for street planting because of its uniformity. Beyond the far outcrop is an outstanding London plane, *Platanus* x *acerifolia,* with an exceptionally symmetrical head. The majestic sweep of low, wide-spreading branches shows what this hybrid can do when given room to develop and allowed to keep its natural form.

In the angle of the Y fork is a small hybrid elm, and behind it a large red oak, this one an open-growing specimen, perhaps more suited to a naturalistic park than the severely regular variety between the outcrops. This oak, like most of the trees in the area, is full of long-dead wood and in urgent need of skilled care.

Now take the left path at the fork and walk downhill towards the playground entrance. To the left of the gate, opposite a stone guardhouse, is a green ash, *Fraxinus pennsylvanica* var. *subintegerrima,* the hairless variety of the red ash. It can be distinguished from the white ash by the green underside of the leaflets and by their short, usually winged stalks.

If you sight from the ash to a lamp post with a police call box and extend the line 5 feet beyond the far side of the asphalt paving, you will come to a shapely small tree with pale gray bark showing a few warty ridges. The leaves have long tapering points and are oblique at the base, with teeth only on the outer margins. If this tree had a crop of witches' brooms, you'd have no difficulty in recognizing it as a hackberry, *Celtis occidentalis*.

Since the leading shoots of immune hackberries are not stunted by disease, the tree grows straight and tall and may reach 100 feet in height. Immunity is inheritable: there is a grove of non-broomy hackberries, adults and saplings, just north of the playground at 81st Street and Central Park West. Hackberries, though members of the elm family, are not subject to Dutch elm disease. Because they endure city conditions and seem to thrive on hardship, immune hackberries are worth trying as street trees.

As you leave the hackberry, walk east into the park to the next lamp post and turn to the right up a gentle slope to meet a most interesting family group, marching two by two like animals into the ark. These are smooth-leafed elms, *Ulmus carpinifolia*. The two-trunked parent must have sprung from twin seeds. Where the trunks compete for growing room, the bark has been squeezed out into a buttress. On the west side, the flange wraps around the trunk like a scarf.

The youngsters, neatly spaced and side by side, originated as suckers from the roots. Their survival suggests that at one time the grass was not mowed close to the tree. Since suckers provide an economical way to increase stock and keep a planting replenished with youthful material, it might be well to preserve a band of meadow grass around especially desirable trees. In addition to possible increase, the buffer zone would prevent the all-too-common bark and root wounds caused by carelessly operated tractor mowers.

Both parent and youngsters are sadly in need of pruning, as dead stubs and branches, long decayed, threaten to hollow the trunks. Elm bark beetles, carriers of the deadly Dutch elm disease fungus, burrow and lay their eggs by choice in the crotches of dead and dying branches, so unpruned elms are doubly menaced.

The question of whether or not to spend major sums of money on elms is a grave one, as it involves factors beyond the Friends' control. If the Park Department were scrupulous about immediate removal of stricken elms, extensive work on elms would unquestionably be justified. However, I saw three large diseased elms in the park in 1969, so nearly dead that they must have been infected a year earlier and perhaps two. They have already hatched their annual brood of beetles and, unless taken down and burned before spring, will release another lethal swarm. A large elm can breed three million beetles.

Can any elm, even the resistant species, withstand such massive invasion every year? On the other hand, if the beetles' favorite egg-laying sites are removed by thorough pruning, may a tree's chances of escaping infection be measurably improved? Can the Park Department be induced to safeguard the park's remaining elms by practicing strict sanitation and thus reduce the annual hatch of spore-carrying beetles?

The emotional impulse is to rush treatment for a tree in obvious need of care. The Friends of Central Park, as trustees of the Camperdown Fund, are obliged to select candidates for salvage on a more sober basis: a careful assessment of a tree's age and importance in the landscape, its vigor, and its site, especially in regard to compaction of the root area. Until some of the foregoing questions about elms are resolved, it seems prudent to devote our general fund to species with a more assured life expectancy. However, contributors who feel that elms are too valuable to abandon without a fight are urged to express their views. If enough donors specify certain elms to be treated, the trees will surely be added to next year's list.

Return to the path and walk east into the park to lamp

post #9315. Forty feet ahead on the right, in the angle of the intersection, is another *U. carpinifolia*, this one with unusually small leaves, hardly larger than those of the Chinese elm. Its trunk and roots are thick with suckers. These adventitious growths have somehow become identified in the public mind with the English elm. They are quite as likely to be found on the smooth-leafed elm. Contrariwise, the English elm may have a perfectly smooth trunk, as we shall see presently.

As you pass lamp post #9313, you will walk through a group of four Austrian pines, *Pinus nigra*, the most durable evergreen conifer in the park. Its rather coarse needles, two to a bundle, may be as long as 6 inches, with a random twist that gives the tree a slightly disheveled look. The Austrian pine is a rough-hewn tree, gaunt and picturesque in age. As a relief from its rather stark outline, it would be pleasant to introduce the silky-tasseled Himalayan pine, *P. wallichiana,* which —surprisingly, in view of its highland origin—does admirably well in low altitudes and under city conditions.

At the edge of the road on the right, across from lamp post #93–13A, is a young *Sophora japonica*, the latest blooming of the peas with sweet-pea-like flowers, a necessary distinction from *Albizzia julibrissin* whose flowers are like shaving brushes. Sophora flower buds are visible in June, open to green-tinged ivory flowers in August and September, and ripen into long, lumpy, pale green pods. In winter the sophora can be recognized by the olive green bark of the shoots, the color persisting in growth three and sometimes four years old.

Cross the road at the traffic light. On the left, 20 feet ahead, is a little-leaf linden, *Tilia cordata*, a European species frequently planted for its dainty foliage and fragrant flowers. Fifty feet north, the same distance from the road, is a large-leafed tree which you might take at a casual glance for the American linden, *T. americana.*

Turn a leaf over and examine it with your hand lens: you will find the underside covered with velvety white hairs. This is the mark of *T. heterophylla,* also a native, but distinct from *T. americana* whose mature leaves are hairless. It will be interesting to see whether this species— possibly repellent to aphids because of its woolly under- wear—is able to survive the cumulative ecological dis- aster that is killing American lindens in the park.

As you approach the bridle path, you will find cock- spur thorns, *Crataegus crus-galli,* on either side. The leaves are elliptical but drawn out into a wedge at the base by wings that sometimes extend all along the leaf- stalk. Margins are toothed except near the base. Profuse clusters of white flowers are followed by persistent fruits, red with tan spots, which measure as much as ¾ inch across.

The number of hawthorn species in northeastern United States is estimated at from 750 to 1200, not count- ing their hybrids. Their identification is an exacting field in which few botanists have chosen to specialize. George Petrides, whose *Field Guide to Trees and Shrubs* is my most used home reference book, illustrates seven leaf forms to show the range of possible variations and then quite sensibly washes his hands of the rest. Except for a few easily recognized kinds, I advise you to follow George Petrides' example.

Cross the bridle path and turn left at lamp post #9321. The massive tree with a major limb dipping to the north is an English elm, *Ulmus procera,* with a smooth trunk showing no burls or suckers. As soon as you touch a leaf, you will feel its characteristic stubble of short wiry hairs. The leaves are softly hairy on the underside and markedly asymmetric at the base.

In the growing season, this giant elm appears in flourishing condition. After the leaves have fallen, it is evident that both divisions of the trunk are hollow. To

51

see how such cavities develop from neglected wounds, look at the low limb from the west. Midway along the horizontal section is an unpainted cut. The exposed wood has dried and cracked, admitting water and offering a haven for fungus spores and insects. In a smaller wound about one third of the distance from the trunk, decay has already entered the heartwood and caused a hollow. The heavy limb, thus weakened, will eventually be lost.

If you walk towards the tennis house, you will see at the southwest corner of the fence a pair of low-headed trees with dramatically fissured bark, pinnately compound leaves, and opposite branches. These are Asian cork trees—not the commercial source of cork which comes from a Spanish oak, *Quercus suber*—but named for the thick corky ridges on the trunk. The undersides of the leaves are densely matted with white hairs, identifying these trees as *Phellodendron amurense* var. *lavallei,* by far the commonest variety in the park. I have found only two stands of the hairless type which you will see on Tours VIII and XI.

The cork tree standing higher on the slope is a female, as you can tell in late summer by its crop of pea-sized fruit, green at first, then ripening to black. If not promptly eaten by birds, the fruit dries and remains on the tree a good part of the winter.

The deeply ridged bark of a fair-sized cork tree should serve as clear distinction from the other commonly seen pinnate leafed, opposite branched genus, the ashes. If you are puzzled by a seedling or if someone sends you a twig to identify, turn back to page 11 for a note on the visibility of the winter buds. If your sample has a leafstalk with a conical base which completely conceals the bud, you can chalk up a cork tree with certainty.

For a discovery that not one in a thousand visitors to Central Park has ever seen, scramble up the slope in the direction of the reservoir and down the other side to the bridle path. There you will find the most enchanting little cast iron bridge in Central Park—or any other, at a wager. The design carries the stamp of gentle Calvert Vaux, combining a sort of softened Gothic with a prediction of Art Nouveau. It is a treasure of the first order, an example of the inexhaustible inventiveness of genius, of a man whose artistic integrity was so steadfast that he couldn't turn out a banal design even for a remote corner of the park.

I had seen this bridge in an old print in the collection of the Museum of the City of New York. There was no note of its location so I made a sketch of it, meaning to find out where it had once stood. It was a shimmering delight to find the endearing little bridge still in existence and still sound, as nearly as can be judged from the outward appearance of the supporting arches. The footpath is now closed because parts of the planking have given way. Park Department workmen are able to replace slats on benches so putting a new deck on this jewel of a bridge is within their capacity. It should by all means be put back in use and given every care needed to preserve it. I shouldn't want to lose it twice.

As you climb the slope to return to the path above the tennis house, you will see an unusually tall hackberry with a balanced head and a most artistically disposed crop of witches' brooms. If you are familiar with Arthur Rackham's imaginative drawings, especially his illustrations for *The Wind in the Willows*, you will recognize the eerie and sometimes menacing figures he revealed in distorted trees: grinning, beak-nosed witches, gnome faces, and bony, pointing fingers.

Here's a bit of fancy to keep you occupied on the way home: suppose you had the power to confer immunity on every hackberry in Central Park. Many people are repelled by witches' brooms, seeing the abnormal growths

53

as unpleasant reminders of disease. This is unarguable: the brooms are caused by a fungus infection. While the disease is not fatal, it certainly stunts the tree and makes it vulnerable to snow damage. On the other hand, would your winter walks in the park have the same zest without the stimulating emphasis of well-broomed hackberries? Remember that you would have walked by an immune specimen near the playground without noticing it.

Have you decided to use your magic cure or to let the witches' brooms remain?

> "We plead for the preservation of largeness and simplicity, for the greatest amount of unobstructed lawn, for trees, and shrubbery, and flowers."
> *Clarence Cook, 1869*

IV

FOREST AND FOUNTAIN

77th Street and Central Park West

Tʜɪs tour embraces the widest possible variety of
scenic experiences from the Ramble's miniature wilderness to the sumptuous formality of the Terrace. On the
way you will find a wealth of exciting plant material,
picturesque mountain scenery, some agreeable places to
enjoy a picnic lunch, and—for the venturesome—a bit
of rock climbing.

Before entering the park, stop for a moment to admire
the magnificent spreading elm in its niche in the parapet
north of the road. The elm's canopy is broader than it is

tall, with a branch hanging free over the wall and dipping well below the tree's root level. If this tree grew in the open, not on a sidewalk, its branches would sweep the ground like a weeping willow's.

The leaves of the elm feel smooth to the fingers so I tentatively marked it down as a smooth-leafed elm, *Ulmus carpinifolia*, subject as always to confirmation by George Kalmbacher.

Before we proceed with the elm, let me introduce Mr. Kalmbacher: taxonomist of the Brooklyn Botanic Garden, my authority for all questions of plant identification, and a stimulating teacher. For my needs, his most valuable gifts are the ability to point out salient distinctions and the knack of translating technical jargon into language an amateur can grasp. I have learned from him never to take a leaf at face value but to examine its underside with a hand lens and to make sure that its measurements fall within stated limits. This is where I had stumbled in the case of the elm.

George, who never makes snap judgments, got out Rehder's *Manual of Cultivated Plants* and his ruler, and found that some of the elm's leaves are 5 inches long, an inch over the accepted 2-4 inch range for *U. carpinifolia*. Some of the leaves also show additional pointed lobes on either side of the central tip. This is a characteristic of the Scotch elm, *U. glabra*, whose leaves may go to 7 inches. Since the influence of Scotch elm is relatively slight, George decided that this tree resulted from backcrossing *Ulmus* x *hollandica* (a *glabra* x *carpinifolia* hybrid) with *carpinifolia*—in other words, it is three parts *carpinifolia* to one part *glabra*.

This elm is planted on filled ground, fully 30 feet above available moisture in the natural grade below. As elms are by nature shallowed rooted, this one must be entirely dependent on rainfall. It is amazing that it has survived successive years of drought. The tree's ability to flourish in such an unfavorable situation is proof of its stamina and the desirability of propagating it. Meanwhile its beautiful dipping branches should be preserved by removing the stunted honey locust that interferes with their graceful sweep.

If it is midsummer when you look over the wall, your eye will be caught by some treelike shrubs with large pleated leaves and showy red berries ripening to black. These are *Viburnum sieboldii*, a Japanese species that makes an exceedingly handsome subject where a bold vertical accent is needed. The red fruit stalks persist after birds have gobbled the berries, making the shrub look as if its twigs were tipped with fine-branched coral.

Starting over Buttress Bridge at the north side, about 10 feet beyond the Naturalists Gate plaque, you will be within arm's length of the upper branches of a maidenhair tree, *Ginkgo biloba*. This bird's view of a young ginkgo is by far the best, as the tree has a long awkward age, with sparse and angular branches like a child's drawing of a tree, and only attains a broad, well-filled head in its late years. This specimen is a female as you can see from the olive-shaped fruit. The fleshy covering of the fruit has an offensive odor, especially when crushed on the sidewalk, so male trees are preferred for street planting. Here the fruit adds greatly to the pattern of the cleft leaves, sea green in color and dusted with a glaucous cast like the bloom on a plum. The ginkgo is no longer known in the wild and has been saved from extinction by the priests of Chinese and Japanese temples—one redeeming item in man's shameful history of destruction.

A bridle path runs under the western arch of Buttress Bridge. The low land just to the east was originally a pond shaped like a butterfly, with a wing on each side of the bridge. To form this small body of water, Olmsted and Vaux utilized one of the five streams that crossed the area of the future park. This one, called the South

Branch of Saw Kill, took its name from a sawmill built in 1664 by Jan Van Bommel at Avenue A. The stream spread into a marshy pond in the hollow where the Museum of Natural History now stands, then entered the park at 75th Street and flowed directly across and out between 74th and 75th Streets. If you consult a map, you will see that the valley which the stream followed was widened to form the Lake. Its lowest point, near Fifth Avenue, became the site of Conservatory Water.

The level of the small pond was maintained by a dam at the mouth of a winding channel leading under Balcony Bridge to the main Lake. It was a serene expanse of water, a haven for swans, ducks, and kingfishers, and a charming complement to the bridle path that followed its western shore. The pond was partly filled in 1880 in an outbreak of panic over malaria, then considered a poisonous emanation rising spontaneously from standing water. Following the policy that one good blunder deserves another, destruction of the watercourse was completed in 1940. Someday, when the city's cultural level rises to appreciation of Olmsted and Vaux's supreme artistic achievement, this body of water may be restored —perhaps by a philanthropist wise enough to know that the most resplendent gift anyone could give the park is a return to its former glory.

The planting on the north side of the road is so dismal that it must be greener on the other side. Let's cross the road to the great rock that curves above the path like a breaking wave. At its east end, about 10 feet from the path, is a small tree with a short, stout trunk dividing in two about 3 feet above ground. This is a native sumach, *Rhus copallina*, with the fitting common name of shining sumach. Its beautifully designed, compact, pinnate leaves are distinguished from those of other sumachs by their usually smooth margins and the instantly recognizable wings along both sides of the central leafstalk. This is

58

one of the strangely overlooked treasures of the plant
world, all too seldom planted in view of its exceptional
merit. For this delight, we must be indebted to a bird-
dropped seed, as it is unlikely that a plant could have
been deliberately set in this narrow crack between rocks.
Every detail of the sumach has interest: the white-furred,
mulberry-colored young shoots and even brighter carmine
buds; the white flowers in midsummer; showy clusters
of velvet-covered crimson fruits; and glorious red-purple
autumn foliage. (In case you are worrying, poison sumach,
like poison ivy, has white berries.) A seedling nearer the
path is being smothered by a forsythia. It should be
rescued and planted where its beauty can be appreciated.

The shrubs on both sides of the road are inexcusably
dull—scanty on this side, ill-chosen and ill-kept on the
other. However, about 25 feet beyond the lamp post
there is a grove of hackberries, *Celtis occidentalis.* These
trees thrive on hardship and are flourishing here in the
parched, compacted soil of a sun-baked, south-facing
slope—a contrast to the bedraggled specimen we saw
on the first tour, with its roots too close to water. The
smooth, pale gray trunks, unfortunately disfigured by
carved initials, and the light green leaves with tapering
points, give an agreeable air of freshness and delicacy
to this otherwise uninviting stretch.

As you cross the road, stop by the traffic light on the
far side. Just to its north is a Turkey oak, *Quercus cerris,*
a Eurasian species which has made itself at home in
Central Park. Leaves may vary in shape but are always
small and neatly designed, with blunt-pointed lobes and
rounded sinuses. This tree is distorted by loss of its
leader and doesn't show the typically erect habit with
heavy horizontal or drooping branches. The bark is
highly individual: rough and corky, with ridges weathered
to gray-white above black crevices. The acorns of the
Turkey oak are of superlative beauty, bullet-shaped,

highly polished, and set in extravagantly fringed cups. You may find a litter of dark brown, woody pompoms on the ground. These are unfertilized female flowers, a good key to identification when acorns are not developed enough to be distinguished.

As you face the water, turn right and walk to lamp post #7507 which stands under a grove of large London planes. The original planting here, according to Peet's chart, was of Turkey oaks and lindens, with only two plane trees as accent on each side of the path leading to the Hernshead. Except for the free-standing specimens that surround an open meadow, Olmsted's directions for woodland plantings are clear: "Individual tree beauty is to be but little regarded, but all consideration is to be given to beauty of groups, passages, and masses of foliage." London planes are too gaudy, too open, too aggressively individual to blend in a harmonious grouping. I'm not suggesting that they be taken down but that no more be planted where they will disrupt a naturalistic landscape. As long as they are here, it would be wise to remove the dead limbs that overhang the path and road. If these rotting branches are not cut flush with the trunk and the wounds kept covered with protective dressing, decay will work back into the heart of the tree and result in a hollow trunk.

Now turn left at the lamp post and walk towards the Lake, to the promontory known as the Hernshead. This secluded area features the delicate iron lace Ladies Pavilion and a monumental rock outcrop. It should be a jewel box setting of choice plants given the most conscientious care. Instead it is a desolate junkpile of third-rate shrubs and broken, sickly trees. Total lack of maintenance of the landscape is matched by neglect of the Ladies Pavilion, abandoned to rust and consequent vandalism. It is a disgrace that this singularly lovely spot should be ignored while money and man hours are diverted from care of the park landscape to the promotion of structural encroachments.

The Ladies Pavilion was designed by Jacob Wrey Mould, whose endlessly inventive play on natural forms enriches the stonework of the Terrace. If Mould's name has been largely eclipsed by the more publicized fame of Olmsted and Vaux, his lavish contribution to the beauty of Central Park was amply appreciated in his day. Clarence Cook, in his *A Description of the New York Central Park*, published in 1869, wrote of Mould: "He has such delight in his art that it is far easier for him to make every fresh design an entirely new one, than to copy something he has made before."

Jacob Wrey Mould's name will soon regain a measure of luster. The Friends of Central Park, unwilling to let his enchanting dollhouse collapse into ruin, are raising money to restore it. Repairing the havoc of total neglect is a costly undertaking, but the fund is growing, and before too long you will read that salvage work has commenced.

The arching branches of a willow, *Salix* x *sepulchralis*, tie the Ladies Pavilion and the rocky headland into a harmonious composition. A small willow has been planted to replace the aging one. Instead of being set in the same relation to the rock, it is placed in the precise spot where it blocks the view from the Pavilion. The willow is a poor specimen, girdled by careless staking in a nursery. It should never have been accepted and can be eliminated without loss. A new willow—an upright, not a weeping form—should be set near the rock where it will frame the view instead of obstructing it.

Walk back through the Pavilion to the low rocks at the northeast point. Here you can marvel at Olmsted and Vaux's ingenuity in weaving the contours of the Lake around existing rock features and their skill in concealing its actual limits. Instead of coming to a visible stop, the

Lake tapers off into little bays and inlets which curve out of sight, suggesting infinite expanses of water just around the bend. In the background, a bridge provides a distant focal point and invites exploration of the half-revealed bay on its far side.

In the early days when ice skating was possible much of the winter, this hill-sheltered cove was known as the Ladies Pond. It was reserved for women and children who felt more secure in its seclusion than among the dashing blades on the open Lake.

Then and now, this is one of the most beautiful pictures in the whole park, satisfying as an entity, rewarding in its details. As your eye traces the shoreline to the left, you first see a promontory clothed in a profuse tangle of willows and shrubs, with the outermost reaching for light over the water. This richly verdant effect embodies Olmsted's ideal. As he wrote from Panama in 1863 to his trusted and esteemed chief landscape gardener, Ignaz Pilat, he realized that he had instinctively been trying to create a tropical atmosphere by the "luxuriant jungled variety and density and intricate abundance of the planting generally of the Lake border and Ramble. . . ."

The inlet to the vanished butterfly pond ran behind this wooded promontory. Beyond it is a barren hillock which shows the effects of overuse in its packed slopes of yellow clay. There is no reason why the unthinking public should be permitted to trample over all parts of the park. It is not doing people a favor to let them destroy what they haven't been educated to value. A fence, well hidden in shrubs, would protect the landward side of the hillock, while all the gaps in the waterside approaches should be filled with thorny shrubs such as the aralia described on page 139. Restoring the massed trees and shrubs that once crowned the Lake's hills and shores

62

stands high on the list of priorities for an enlightened adminstrator.

Let's return now to the path along the road and turn right at lamp post #7507, stopping on Balcony Bridge for a look across the water to the Ramble's massive, glacier-polished cliffs and thickly wooded slopes. The naturalness of the scene is marred by a conspicuous concrete retaining wall. A sensitive designer would have faced the concrete with native rock. Even so, its glaring artificiality can easily be camouflaged by a dense planting of shrubs and vines.

At the far end of Balcony Bridge, take the right-hand path and turn right again at #7728 to cross Bank Rock Bridge. Stop on the bridge a moment to admire the weeping willows whose trailing branches mask the north end of the cove, now silted and used only by urchins who catch crayfish in the murky water.

Before we plunge into the forest, turn back for a look at the Hernshead where on sunny days people lie draped over the rock like seals on a ledge.

As you come off the bridge, stop to look at the large tree to the right. This is one of the easiest of the compound leafed trees to recognize. First of all, its alternate branching and the oversize terminal leaflets mark it as a hickory. The half-inch buds, dusted with golden yellow, are the key to the bitternut hickory, *Carya cordiformis.* The husk of the nut has four ridges or wings on the outer half. Presumably the even larger tree across the path is also a bitternut—both have mostly seven leaflets—but branches are too high to permit examining the bud.

Starting at the end of the bridge, take the path uphill to the left, go up the stairs on the right, and take another right turn around #7703. The large tree across the path on the left, with a younger one at its foot, is *Sophora japonica,* called scholar or pagoda tree. This is a giant member of the pea family, valued for its clean, delicate foliage and the great clusters of milky-white flowers, slightly tinged with green, which are freely produced over a long period in late summer.

Walk ahead onto the stone arch which looks from below like a giant's keyhole or the narrow gateway to Petra, the storied city carved from stone. Two of the Ramble's most spectacular rock formations are visible from this vantage point: a sheer cliff below to the right and an even steeper outcrop beyond the steps to the left. By all means explore the lower level of this dramatic area on another occasion. It is charged with exciting surprises.

Below the far left end of the stone arch stands a huge upright rock. This formed one pier of the landward entrance to a cave or tunnel created by Olmsted and Vaux by roofing a narrow crevice with massive rocks. The far side opened on a small inlet from the Lake. This must have provided a thrilling stage setting for junior pirates, smugglers, and Indians—and grown-ups too, as you can see in old prints. Both entrances have been sealed, and the landward approach obliterated with earth.

It took an afternoon in the Print Room of the Museum of the City of New York and another in the library of the New York Historical Society to reconstruct a trip through the Cave. Clarence Cook gives a vivid contemporary account of the delicious tremors that accompanied the venture.

> "A steep path skirting a bank thickly set with rhododendrons, laurel, and azaleas . . . leads to the foot of a large mass of rock, where a sharp turn to the left brings us to the Cave. At first, its entrance is very dark, and causes many a palpitation in tender breasts, but a few steps bring us to the light, and in a moment we find ourselves looking out upon a peaceful cove, an arm of the Lake. . . ."

64

The perils of this entrance must have been purely imaginary, as an old print shows an unaccompained lady in a sweeping gown—certainly not costumed for rock climbing—about to descend an easy flight of broad stone steps.

Old photographs show boats approaching the mouth of the Cave from the south but because of the shadowing overhang, it was impossible to tell how far the water extended into the Cave. A detailed engraving in Cook's priceless record cleared up the puzzle. Those who entered by land came out on a narrow apron of flat rock that served as a boat landing. At this point, the explorer could return by the easy route or climb a steep and hazardous stairway up the face of the cliff to the right.

The landward entrance has been buried but we can still taste a little of the drama of the seaward approach. Go down the steps at the end of the stone arch, turn right at #7627, and go around to #7623A where you can see a narrow flight of steps chiseled out of the living rock. The steps are slippery with silt and there is no handrail so don't try the descent unless you are agile and sure-footed. I don't know how compelling the illusion would be in daylight but at night the huge mass of the outthrust lintel seems to soar overhead like a monstrous wing against the sky. This is an irresistible adventure which should be made available to everyone, with the landward route usable for those who can't negotiate the dangerous stairs.

Who'll form a committee to open the Cave?

When you've caught your breath after the climb to the cliff top, retrace your steps to the end of the stone arch and follow the path as it curves to the right through a grove of black locusts, with a large one behind #7629. You should recall from the first tour the thin-textured, rounded leaflets and the strongly grooved bark overlaid with ridges in high relief.

The understory plants that cover this slope are the native witchhazel, *Hamamelis virginiana,* irregularly arching shrubs or small trees. The leaves are large, wavy edged, oblique at the base, and unequal in size and shape on either side of the midvein. The witchhazel's charming eccentricity is its choice of flowering time, in late November just as its clear yellow leaves begin to fall. The flowers are not spectacular, being little spidery tufts of straw yellow ribbons, but even a modest show of color is welcome in the gray season. The seed capsules are visible much of the summer and are quite distinctive: thimble-sized urns, pale green, felt covered, with beak-like projections on the lid. Ripe seeds are expelled with stinging force, sometimes to a distance of 30 feet, a trait that earned the witchhazel one of its common names, Snapping Alder.

As you walk ahead, take the next right turn under a grove of black cherries—a flurry of robins and thrushes if migration time is near—and pause at lamp post #7633. The witchhazels here are more accessible than those previously seen, offering a good opportunity to look for the curious fruit capsules—and, perhaps, get pelted by a barrage of seeds. The "witch" in witchhazel has nothing to do with the Hallowe'en variety, but derives from an OE word meaning "pliant" or "whiplike" which survives also in "switch" and in "wych-elm," one of the common names of the Scotch elm, *Ulmus glabra.*

Beyond the end of the fence, in the angle of the path that branches to the right, is a group of *Viburnum tomentosum,* the double-file viburnum, which takes its name from its handsome white flower clusters set alternately in two rows along the arching canes. The site is too shaded for free flowering but a well-placed specimen in dazzling mid-May bloom is strikingly beautiful and is sometimes mistaken for a flowering dogwood.

In the opposite corner of this right-hand path, which

66

we'll take presently, stands a large tulip tree. You will recognize it at once by the blunt leaf with its shallow wedge-shaped indentation. The many dead branches on this tree are evidence of severe root injury suffered after the porous gravel paths were converted to suffocating asphalt. It is not generally understood that roots need air as well as water, and that the root run, which extends at least as far as the ends of the branches, must be kept open to absorb rain and to permit the exchange of air and waste gases.

Take a few steps along the right-hand path to see the gracefully arching, three-trunked shrub behind the tulip tree. This is the black haw, *Viburnum prunifolium*, one of our most distinguished native shrubs, clean leafed, elegant in habit, and turning a glorious rose-red in autumn. You can recognize this viburnum in winter by the bark which breaks into small tortoise-shell plates, a replica in miniature of the bark of flowering dogwoods. There are black haws on both sides of the path here, and as you walk forward between them, you have an example of ideal woodland understory planting—in sharp contrast to the stiff, ungainly privet behind lamp post #7637 on the left.

On the right there is a flat ledge with a great boulder on it. Sit here for a moment to recreate in fancy the splendor of the scene as Olmsted and Vaux devised it. An inlet from the Lake wound between the ledge at your feet and the rock-strewn slope on the other side, and led to the mouth of the Cave at the far right. Remove the tumbledown willows that block the view, clothe the hillsides in dense shrubbery, train vines over the barren rocks around the Cave, and you can imagine yourself in a mountain gorge. The scale is miniature but so consistent that the illusion is projected without flaw. This is a Thomas Cole painting translated into three dimensions. "My picture is all alive," Olmsted wrote, "its very essence

68

is life, human and vegetable." Restoring this scene to life is another imperative item on the list of priorities for the reconstruction of Central Park.

When you are rested, walk on down the slope to the next big tree near the path on the right. This is a shagbark hickory, *Carya ovata*. The bark of this species warps and peels like the shingles of an old weathered barn. This characteristic and the number of leaflets (usually five) will be all the identification you need. If you are lucky enough to find a nut overlooked by squirrels, you will enjoy the sweet, full-flavored meat. Indians used to steep the crushed nuts in boiling water to extract the oil. The fluid, rich as cream and prized for its use in cooking, was called *pocohicora* by the Algonquins: it is from this nut-milk that we derive our name for the tree.

As the path bends ahead, some 25 feet before you reach lamp post #7531, you will see a compound leafed tree on your right. The three terminal leaflets are larger than the basal ones, the mark of a hickory. One look at the elongated, bright yellow buds, and you can have no hesitation in declaring it a bitternut. Note the domed rock on the opposite side of the path, with a folded overhang that looks almost like drapery.

Continue down the steps, cross the plank bridge, and look up the ravine, a miniature mountain torrent. Appreciation of native scenery, especially in its wild and rough forms, was slow to develop in America. The colonist, the frontiersman, the homesteader viewed forests as wasted land and trees as an obstacle to be cleared away for farming. It was not until much of our wilderness had been destroyed that its value was recognized. Thomas Cole, founder of the Hudson River School of painting in the early nineteenth century, was a major force in awakening a sense of national pride in the scenic grandeur of the Hudson Valley and adjacent highlands. This little ravine, in reduced scale and reversed from

69

left to right, is a startling likeness of the scene painted by Asher Durand in which Thomas Cole is pointing out to William Cullen Bryant the glories of a mountain stream in the Catskills.

With uncanny prescience, Olmsted wrote in 1859:

> "The time will come when New York will be built up, when all the grading and filling will be done, and when the picturesquely varied, rocky formation of the Island will have been converted into foundations for rows of monotonous straight streets, and piles of erect, angular buildings. There will be no suggestion left of its present varied surface, with the single exception of the few acres contained in the Park. . . . It therefore seems desirable to interfere with the easy, undulating outlines and picturesque, rocky scenery as little as possible."

By Olmsted's express direction, the banks of the ravine should be a tumbling profusion of greenery with all broken rock concealed and only the massive ledges visible. Instead, much of the shrubbery has been stripped away, leading to erosion and then an effort to hold the soil with cribbing, a routine that is doggedly repeated in Central and Prospect Park with nothing learned from the unfailingly disastrous results. Where plants *should* be cleared away, a lack of discriminating taste lets them remain. Here a thicket of the insufferable polygonum blots out the lower end of the stream. The crowning idiocy is the planting of a willow right in the mouth of the gorge where, if it escapes deserved vandalism, it will totally block the view. Bungled work of this sort was forcefully ascribed by Olmsted to "IGNORANCE. . . . complete, blind ignorance—of the principles, even of the motives and objects" of landscape architecture. Even if this were the only instance of hackwork in the whole park, it is sufficient reason to insist on supervision of every detail of planting by a highly qualified landscape architect.

70

Forest and Fountain

If you are sure-footed, climb among the rocks to the right of the stream to see what is hidden behind the misplaced plant barrier. There is a secluded little glade, a most inviting spot for a picnic, on the far side of the bridge that spans the stream.

The waterfall, a mere trickle, should foam over the rocks in much greater volume. If the Gill that feeds it doesn't have enough flow, an additional supply could be piped in at the top to make a convincing cataract. There is a crudely cemented, and leaking, dam to be removed. However, the flaws that diminish the scene are superficial and easily reversed. The basic concept of the plan, by which a sloping outcrop has been transformed into a mountain gorge, has been carried out in spectacular style. With a small expenditure of money and a larger measure of brains, the ravine can again be made one of the chief scenic attractions of Central Park.

When you return to the footpath, take a right turn as it swings to follow the shoreline. Opposite lamp post #7523, you have an opportunity to examine a sour gum, *Nyssa sylvatica*, at close range. You will recall seeing a typically single trunked specimen across the Pool on the first tour. In this one, the trunk divides in two about shoulder height. The leaves are obovoid—that is, a reversed egg with the stem on the smaller end—and not especially distinctive until they start turning color in late summer, at first just a scattering of leaves, then a branch or two, ending in a positive conflagration of burnished scarlet or claret red.

The huge brown-trunked tree ahead on the right, near the next lamp post, is a tulip tree nearly dead of old age. In accordance with accepted policies of foresighted forest management, a replacement should be planted nearby.

Across the path from the tulip tree, with its roots almost touching a bench support, is a sweet gum, *Liquid-*

71

ambar styraciflua. Its star-shaped leaves are unfailingly clean and ornamental, and its autumn coloration is rich and varied. The sweet gum can't be overpraised. Its head has solidity without heaviness, unlike, for instance, the coarse American linden. Sweet gums should be used extensively to reinforce weak plantations of locusts, hybrid elms, and pin oaks, especially those around the borders of meadows where density of foliage and heavy shadows are wanted.

Waterside trees are well represented along this shore and should be supplemented by an equally rich variety of moisture-loving shrubs. Clethra, *Rhododendron viscosum*, and *Magnolia virginiana* would make this woodland walk a bower of midsummer bloom and fragrance, with fothergilla and *Oxydendrum arboreum* planted near the water to cast their brilliantly colored reflections in autumn.

Ten feet before you reach the next bench on the left, stop to examine the small tree with boldly striped bark in shades of gray. This is a hornbeam which bore no fruit in 1969. It is tentatively identified as an American (*Carpinus caroliniana*) because of its tiny buds, ⅛ inch or less, and the generally delicate, fine-twigged character of its growth. If it produces fruit clusters another year, you can check them with the dimensions given on page 8 and confirm or correct the identification accordingly.

Some young sassafras saplings (*Sassafras albidum*) hang their branches over the back of the bench, low enough so that you can observe their green stems and the varying shape of the leaves—some simple ovals, some with an extra lobe like a mitten, and some with two. When Olmsted wrote of "the childish playfulness and profuse careless utterance of Nature" he was enraptured by the luxuriance of the tropics, but his delight in the endless inventiveness of nature might apply with equal aptness to the fanciful sassafras.

Behind the next bench is another non-fruiting hornbeam, again provisionally set down as the American. The spiral ridges of the trunk look like muscles in stress.

Pass lamp post #7417 and the next bench. Beyond are some taller sassafras trees which show their typical irregular branching habit and roughly furrowed bark— not in continous ridges like the black locust's, but in a broken pattern. The green twigs, which keep their color in winter, are a helpful means of recognition.

Just beyond lamp post #7415 and nearer the water, about 2 yards from the path, is a willow oak, *Quercus phellos.* This is one of our most beautiful and distinctive native oaks, now being tested as a street tree. Willow oak bark is dark and fairly smooth, and the leaves so long and slender that you may have to hunt for an acorn to convince yourself that this is truly an oak and not a willow. In any case, if you examine the leaves closely, you will find that the edges are not toothed as a willow's are. Young leaves have a bristle projecting from the tip, a token of the willow oak's place in the red oak section.

Follow the walk around to the right and stop just beyond #7315 to look at the piled-up rocks on both sides of the path. These rocks were intended to support vines as vertical accents to break up the flatness of the shoreline, not to be exposed in all their artifice. The surviving wisteria on the right could easily be trained around and over the balanced rock to make it look like a solid, natural headland. Behind the rock is a sweet gum with a heartening family of saplings springing from its roots.

Bow Bridge itself is framed by a sparse thicket of *Viburnum prunifolium,* rapidly being choked by the park's most damaging weed, *Polygonum cuspidatum.* Still on the right, some low-branched black locusts will give you in mid- or late May an intoxicating wave of fragrance.

Bow Bridge, designed by Calvert Vaux, is one of the few cast iron bridges still in existence, and one of the most graceful. Clarence Cook described it in 1869:

> "It is made entirely of wrought iron, resting on two abutments of stone, one of the ends being placed upon cannon-balls, in order to allow for the necessary expansion and contraction with heat and cold. At the ends of the bridge, over the abutments, are placed iron vases which, in summer, are kept filled with flowering plants, and it is not without reason that it is generally considered the handsomest of all bridges in the Park."

All the more shame, then, that Bow Bridge has been allowed to lapse into a shocking state of disrepair. Because joints were not kept sealed, moisture has entered the hollow members and rust is eating the structure from within. The only maintenance in recent years, except for paint, is a plywood patch on the worn timber flooring. The abandonment to rust of this historic and uniquely beautiful landmark is another example of warped priorities: vast sums are spent to stage concerts that exploit the park for commercial advertising and to operate a roofless Broadway theater, while hardly a cent is devoted to the preservation of the park's real treasures.

A private benefactor who undertakes the restoration of Bow Bridge will do more than preserve one of the park's integral features. His gift may divert donors from burying the park under structural monuments and turn them instead to erasing the scars that ignorance and neglect have inflicted on Olmsted and Vaux's world-renowned landscape.

As you walk over the bridge, you will see a catalpa, *Catalpa bignonioides,* hanging over the water at the far right side. Its huge heart-shaped leaves are arranged in a whorl of three around the stem. In mid-June it bears upright clusters of large tubular flowers with a flaring lower lip, pure white except for purple and gold markings in the throat. The fruits are slender cylindrical pods as much as 18 inches long. Shreds of these beans often persist all winter and afford an easy means of identification.

In the angle of the path as it turns right is a European weeping birch, *Betula pendula*. Its bark may not be as dazzling as that of our paper birch but its habit is more graceful. It is tolerant of heat and seems to resist the borers and fungus that make short work of paper birches in hot climates.

Directly ahead in the Y fork, behind #7301, is a monumental bur or mossycup oak, *Quercus macrocarpa*. The leaves are round lobed, indicating that it belongs to the white oak group, and are divided almost in half by a deep sinus. Acorn cups are thimble-shaped, covering about two-thirds of the nut, and are fringed at the lip.

This superb tree is part of the original planting. Take a good look at it. It hasn't long to live. Erosion has exposed the roots; trampling feet and fire have destroyed their bark covering; decay has rotted the roots and is far advanced in the base of the trunk. As soon as the threat was apparent, this irreplaceable tree should have been protected by a fence or, better, surrounded with an impenetrable thicket of cockspur thorns or *Rosa multiflora* or the steel-spined hardy orange, *Poncirus trifoliata*.

If all the Park Department's crimes of omission were drawn up, this tree, wantonly sacrificed to indifference and irresponsibility, would be the place to nail them. Only a professionally trained horticultural director for each of the Olmsted parks can reverse such shameful neglect of the treasures of the landscape; only persistent, organized public demand will bring about the administrative changes that must be made if the parks are to survive.

With a last look of regret at the doomed bur oak, take the left fork of the path and walk to lamp post #7305. On either side of it is a narrow-growing ginkgo with branches erect and held close to the trunk in a manner quite different from the normal, spreading ginkgo we saw from Buttress Bridge. Trees having this columnar form are described as fastigiate. The most familiar example is the Lombardy poplar, a fastigiate variety of the black poplar.

The tree on the point with its roots touching the water is a poplar whose identification took up an entire working lunchtime in the Boat House. It has a flattened leafstalk set at right angles to the plane of the leaf, a feature shared by several poplars and causing the familiar flashing and trembling of the leaves. For the rest, the pinning down of a tree that doesn't fit any simple category is a lengthy job, far too exacting to tackle near the end of a long walk. Mark it down as *Populus* x *canadensis,* a hybrid between the common cottonwood and black popular, and look for the analysis on a later walk (page 110).

Continue along the shore to lamp post #7229. Below it, almost at the water's edge, is a large tree with drooping lower branches. You have learned that this is the mark of the pin oak, but look again: the leaves of this tree have rounded lobes, not pointed ones, so it must belong to the white oak group. It is a swamp white oak, *Quercus bicolor,* which differs from the white oak in having shallower sinuses—sometimes merely wavy edges—and in broadening on the outer half instead of tapering. The underside of the leaf is thickly haired. The acorns of the white oak are unique in being borne in pairs on a stalk as long as 3 inches. To check your memory, the next large tree on the left is a pin oak which you will remember for its small, sharp-pointed leaves and airy canopy.

Since this is a tree and landscape book, I must limit my admiration for the superlative Terrace designed by Calvert Vaux and Jacob Wrey Mould. It is fully described and pictured by old engravings in Henry Hope Reed's *Central Park: A History and a Guide.*

If you walk up the open flight of stairs to the right, you can see from the top the bronze angel hovering between sky and water. As you face the Lake, look up into the branches of a giant *Paulownia tomentosa,* called Empress Tree or Empress-of-China though it was named for the daughter of a Russian czar. It stands just outside the flanking wall of the stairs to your left, with one branch overhanging an urn on the parapet. The paulownia is the fourth of the opposite branching trees indicated in the code word DAMPh. It is a soft wooded, rapid growing, short lived tree, yet this specimen is unmistakably indicated in Peet. Despite extraordinary age, faulty pruning, and untreated wounds, this venerable tree still produces a plentiful crop of large, tubular, violet flowers in mid-May.

The paulownia belongs to the same order, but not the same family, as the catalpa, and resembles it to a confusing extent. The paulownia, however, can be identified in winter by its upright panicles of nodding, tan, felt-covered buds, the austere motif of the Chinese imperial crest. The fruit is a brown woody capsule resembling a pecan shell in shape, but full of tiny papery seeds like goldfish food. If you see any of these distinguishing features, you will have no difficulty in separating the paulownia from the white flowered, long-beaned catalpa.

An enormous English elm, *Ulmus procera,* stands between the footpath and the road. Habit and leaf form are so much like the smooth-leafed elm, *U. carpinifolia,* that you must examine a leaf to tell them apart. The branches of this specimen are too high to reach but if a squirrel has nipped off a twig, you can verify the identification. The upper surface of the English elm leaf bears a stubble of short stiff hairs, readily seen under a hand lens and feeling like sandpaper to a fingertip.

The Mall was originally roofed with a cathedral vault of American elms, all lost to the ravages of Dutch elm disease. While the stocky, low branched English elm is no substitute for the soaring American, it has a solid majesty that complements the architectural grandeur of the Terrace. Ancient trees and richly carved stonework are components of a master design, the harmoniously blended artistry of three singularly gifted men: Olmsted, Vaux, and Mould.

Central Park was designated a National Historical Landmark in 1965. Official recognition of its status as an inviolable part of our cultural heritage was achieved largely through the initiative of the late Robert Kennedy. It is fitting that the largest single contribution to the 1969 tree salvage program of the Friends of Central Park was given in memory of Senator Kennedy. The gift from the Josephine B. Crane Foundation was made with the expressed hope that it will form the nucleus of a continuous working fund to honor Senator Kennedy's devoted service in preserving Central Park.

"A more unpromising locality was never given to any Adam to make an Eden of, and few persons who have not watched the progress of the Park from its commencement, can fully understand that its present condition is almost entirely an artificial product. Nature having done almost nothing, art had to do all."

Clarence Cook, 1869

V

EAST
MEADOW

*97th Street
and Fifth Avenue*

THE discovery of East Meadow is one of the rewards of exploring Central Park. When I first came upon it in July of 1969, I was overjoyed to recognize Olmsted's ideal park scene, a pastoral landscape:

> "A broad stretch of slightly undulating meadow without defined edge, its turf lost in a haze of the shadows of scattered trees where the imagination, looking into the soft commingling lights and shadows and fading tints of color of the back ground would have encouragement to extend these purely rural conditions indefinitely."

In just four months, the quality of the landscape has been impaired. Accident, neglect, and deliberate mutilation have taken toll of vital trees and shrubs. What has happened to East Meadow holds true throughout Central Park.

As you enter East Meadow from Fifth Avenue just north of the 97th Street transverse, the first tree you see on your right, about 30 feet behind lamp post #9702, is a silver maple, *Acer saccharinum*. The leaves are silvery on the underside, sharply toothed, and with deep sinuses that undercut the base of the central lobe. Some forms have leaves so intricately slashed and fringed that they resemble those of Japanese cut-leaf maples. The bark is pale gray and, on mature trunks, peels in flakes somewhat like those of a white oak's, but of course the maple's opposite branching will prevent any confusion.

Silver maples were once used extensively as street trees but their soft, easily rotted wood and habit of dropping large branches without warning have earned them the reputation of being dangerous—so much so that their use as street trees is banned in some communities. This specimen, though young, already shows a telltale decayed stub on the north side about 25 feet above ground.

As you walk forward towards the intersection of the paths, you will see a smooth-leafed elm, *Ulmus carpinifolia*, on the right. Its trunk carries a number of burls which, to a novice, may look like an alarming disease. Burls are not caused by infection or injury but by erratic buds—adventitious buds, in the jargon—which somehow got trapped below the surface and, though buried, are still trying to force their way out. When they succeed, they appear as suckers such as we saw on the whiskery elm near the start of Tour II.

The fine grained, tightly interwoven tissues of burls produce beautifully patterned veneers. Elm and walnut burl veneers were especially popular at the start of the eighteenth century: they add richness and elegance to furniture of the Queen Anne period. In the early days of the American colonies, Indians taught the settlers to use burls for household woodenware such as bowls and mortars. Because of the interlocking grain, bowls made of burl wood won't crack or split, even when used to hold liquid or when pounded with a pestle to crush dried herbs and spices.

Ahead, by lamp post #9710, you may see the stump of a magnificent elm which, in July, commanded the south end of the meadow. It had a regal canopy of arching branches, broad enough to enclose the border with foliage, hiding the paved path in a pattern of sun and shade, and revealing only a glimpse of the shrub barrier along the transverse road. My note of early July records a hollow and evidence of decay in a large limb reaching to the west, but there was no trace of Dutch elm disease, so shockingly advertised by a sudden yellowing of leaves and—as the infection progresses—the brown, dried leaves that hang on dead twigs. I believe that the tree may have lost its top in a strangely localized windstorm which severely damaged a number of trees in this small area.

It is perhaps too late to wonder whether reinforcing the spreading branches with cables might have saved this glorious elm from destruction. It is of immediate concern to have the remaining giants secured against similar loss. As Hermann Merkel wrote in his 1927 survey of the needs of Central Park, "Every large tree should be considered as a priceless object since it cannot be replaced."

It will take an effort of imagination to visualize East Meadow as it was before the loss of this great elm. Nothing, however, can bring home so powerfully the crucial role of mature trees in the landscape and the imperative need of preserving them through optimum care.

Only a stunted American linden with a deformed leader remains at this end of the meadow, an object lesson in the folly of retaining sickly trees. The question of what to do with a substandard tree or shrub can be solved by applying a simple formula: "If I saw it in a nursery, would I buy it?" Obviously, if it isn't good enough to buy, it isn't worth keeping.

If the crippled linden had been removed and replaced with a sound, strong-growing tree, the loss of the great elm would not be so devastating. As it is, replanting must start from scratch. Rather than wait a hundred years for a single tree to reach maturity, a grove of sweet gums might be used to fill the void at the end of the meadow.

Just before reaching the row of benches, let's walk up the slope to the planting along the edge of the transverse road. The shrubs along the border are *Photinia villosa,* a first-rate plant with flamboyant yellow to lacquer-red autumn color. Its showy red berries ripen just in time to provide journey cake for birds about to take off on their southward flight. Young shoots and the underside of the leaves are covered with fine down, as the name *villosa* indicates. The photinia is an oriental shrub but is quite as much at home in a naturalistic setting as the *Viburnum sieboldii* we have seen previously. Like the viburnum, it is of generous proportion, vigorous, clean, and trouble free, and thus a better choice for park planting than garden subjects such as aphid-attracting mock oranges. The photinias have been planted in a straight row—a staggered line would be more natural and effective—but their billowy habit helps to overcome the hedgerow effect.

Behind the photinias, on the edge of the road, is a line of young Chinese elms, *Ulmus parvifolia,* distinguished from other elms by their tiny leaves and mottled bark. The ancient Chinese elm we saw at the start of Tour II has reddish bark; these have the commoner gray tones. The filmy heads of Chinese elms make them a poor choice for screen planting. Olmsted knew that only dense growth could block an undesirable view and stimulate

82

the imagination. "No one," he wrote, "looking into a closely grown wood, can be certain that at a short distance back there are not glades or streams. . . ."

Nobody can have any illusion about what lies behind this barrier. As if the loss of the great elm was not disaster enough, the already meager planting was deliberately thinned in October. A number of black cherries were cut down; others, and a sycamore maple sapling, were stripped of their lower branches. Gaps in the barrier now reveal the rush and noise of traffic and promote a free circulation of carbon monoxide.

The Park Department's zeal in hacking off low branches appears to be an uncontrollable nervous tic, unrelated to any consideration of the natural habit of a plant or its function in the landscape. The old excuse that stripping the park enhances public safety has been repudiated by Commissioner Heckscher and the police, yet the mindless vandalism continues. A direct approach makes better sense: retire slow, cumbersome police cars and horses and put alert, well instructed patrolmen on scooters to zip constantly through the park.

Return to the path and walk ahead to the intersection, passing to the right of the numberless lamp post. Pause under the magnificent smooth-leafed elm to admire its canopy of wide-spread, arching limbs and their animated pattern against the sky. If you can imagine holding your arms out horizontally from the shoulders for a hundred years, and multiply the weight of arms by the bulk of the tree's massive limbs, you will have some estimate of the strain exerted at the crotch where branch joins trunk. Since this elm is an exposed position, on a rise open to the full sweep of wind across the meadow, it was chosen for protective treatment by the Friends of Central Park in 1969.

Members of the Altrusa Club of New York, an international service club of executive business and professional women, learned of the need to safeguard this superlative tree and adopted it as one of their civic projects. Through the club's generous contribution to the Camperdown Fund, the tree was cleared of dead wood and given deep root feeding by the Bartlett Company. The exposed wood of old cuts, correctly made and partially healed but not kept painted, was dressed with protective coating. Most important, a network of cables was installed to distribute the immense weight of the horizontal branches over the entire canopy, much as the roadbed of a suspension bridge is supported by cables over the piers.

The 1969 tree salvage program dealt with trees located from 72nd Street to 100th. At 72nd, 84th, and 85th, people stopped briefly to stare but shied off when I approached to tell them of the Friends' program. Nearby residents who walk children and dogs in East Meadow showed more lively interest than those of all other areas put together.

During the two days in which the Bartlett men worked in Altrusa's elm, a number of men and women saw the truck, the ladder, the heaps of dead branches on the ground, and rushed up in dismay, crying, "Oh, you aren't cutting down that wonderful old tree, are you?" Their relief at learning that the work was to protect, not destroy, the tree was most heartening in its degree of concern and involvement. As word of the opportunity to participate gets round, East Meadow may well be the first section of Central Park to be restored to its original splendor through public action by individuals and by organizations such as the Altrusa Club.

As you follow the path to the right around the edge of the meadow, you will see the remains of a remarkable grove of beeches—over forty of them, if Peet's dots can be taken as an accurate count. These are European beeches, *Fagus sylvatica*, easily distinguished from the American beech by the toothless margin of the leaf. By mid-July the nuts are well developed and quite conspicu-

84

ous in their green husks with rusty-brown spines. The four-parted husks open in September to shed their two triangular nuts, tightly packed with their broadest sides touching. The inside of the husk has a satin-smooth finish, a very pleasing tactile contrast to the rough exterior. If you put one in your pocket, you'll find your fingers returning to it again and again.

The beech grove in its prime must have offered an almost architectural shelter with trunks like gray stone columns supporting a solid canopy of foliage. In a plantation as close as this, the lower branches inevitably die of shading. Dead branches either were not removed promptly or the wounds were not kept sealed with dressing: most of the surviving trees show cavities and extensive decay. Only one beech has been planted as replacement. Instead, a scattering of silver-leaf lindens has been dropped into the meadow. These are splendid trees in every way but they do not contribute to the unified impression of the all-beech grove. Charles Eliot Norton, eminent critic and professor of art history at Harvard University, called Olmsted "the greatest artist that America has yet produced." When the caretakers of Olmsted's masterpiece arbitrarily alter his design, the result falls short of genius.

On the left beyond lamp post #9812 is a rock outcrop furnished with a dying, roots-in-the-air black cherry and a fringe of yellow grass. The planting on top of the hillock and along the road is pitifully meager, too thin to screen cars or to make an imposing backdrop for the meadow. The scene has been further impoverished by loss of a large green ash which stood by the roadside and helped enclose the meadow. It disappeared between July and September.

The hill might be crowned by Himalayan pines, *Pinus wallichiana,* with sweeping branches and long tassels of soft, pendent needles. Since this is one of the relatively few needle-leafed evergreens that can thrive in the city, it is regrettable that it hasn't been used freely in the park. Another worthy evergreen, similarly overlooked, is the firethorn, *Pyracantha coccinea* and its somewhat hardier variety, *P. c. lalandii.* Vivid orange-red berries make a striking display in early autumn and are prized by migrating birds. Used in quantity, these two evergreens would make an effective visual barrier against automobile traffic as well as a rich background for flowering shrubs such as *Corylopsis sinensis* and *Prunus triloba,* broad-based plants that hug the ground and give a feeling of stability impossible to achieve with leggy garden subjects. A massed group of large-scale material would accentuate the monumental quality of the outcrop and give it sufficient importance to balance the huge elms on the east and southwest margins. These suggested enrichments and the restoration of border and background plantings at both ends of East Meadow would be a worthy project for persons who share Olmsted's vision of a verdant haven in the midst of a great city.

Beyond the crest of the outcrop, about 60 feet past lamp post #9918, stands a tall honey locust, *Gleditsia triacanthos.* Ferocious branching spines, often with three points, measure as much as 3 inches in length. The bark is teakwood brown or nearly black, tight fitting, and relatively smooth, with some flaking or peeling on mature trunks. Leaves are much smaller, deeper green, and heavier in texture than the black locust seen at the Pool and later in the Ramble. Flowers of the honey locust are greenish yellow and hardly noticeable. They are followed by the most distinctive feature of the tree, fantastically twisted pods sometimes 18 inches long. The green pods, visible in midsummer, turn a rich, polished chestnut brown before they fall, when they are avidly collected by children and flower arrangers.

Walk forward to the drinking fountain, turn sharp left

87

at the intersection and walk ahead to lamp post #0026. About 30 feet behind it is a little hackberry with an intricate filigree of witches' brooms. The circling branches are in perfect balance, not static but with a sense of arrested motion, like a dancer poised in an arabesque.

Farther to the left on the rise are two oaks. The deeply ridged, corky bark, black with ash gray ridges, and the heavy, low branching habit should enable you to recognize a Turkey oak without needing to examine its leaves or look for its bullet-shaped acorns in their fringed cups.

In contrast to the quiet beauty of East Meadow, look across the road to the ruins of North Meadow. By Olmsted's careful plan, the natural scenery was unmarred by any man-made feature, even the archways being placed out of the line of vision. It is now a no man's land of chain link fencing and dusty bare earth.

In the early days of Central Park, the Commissioners were keenly aware of their responsibility to preserve the beauty of the landscape for the majority of visitors. To save the turf on the principal meadows—the Playground, Green, and North Meadow—ball playing was restricted to schoolboys and permitted only at the discretion of the Superintendent. Clarence Cook wrote in 1869:

> "It is used three days in each week by such boys as are thought by their teachers to have earned the privilege by good conduct. This is a reward of merit that the boys appreciate, and it has thus far proved a great incentive to study and to good conduct."

Unhappily, this guarded concession to organized sport proved impossible to enforce. In 1875 Olmsted wrote:

> "There are as many as 50 and sometimes as many as 200 full grown men who have been on the green at once, most of them rude fellows, who by main force take possession of considerable parts of it, practically excluding the boys and depriving them of their legal rights."

Olmsted's objection to letting any group usurp park land, thus excluding the general public, rests on a fundamental tenet of the park's charter. Central Park was conceived on democratic principles. The Commissioners proclaimed in their second annual report, dated January 1, 1859, that "the primary purpose of the Park is to provide the best practicable means of healthful recreation for the inhabitants of all classes." Olmsted added, "It is of great importance as the first real park made in this country—a democratic development of the highest significance."

Central Park is clearly dedicated to the free open use of all people without exception or favor. Fencing off acres of park land for the use of special groups is a denial of the basic premise on which the park is founded.

As the city's population grows unchecked, the need to preserve and increase urban open space becomes more and more crucial. When existing land is withdrawn from general use, the rest of the park suffers from intensified overcrowding. Is it conscionable to let the southern part of Central Park be trampled to death when the great sweep of North Meadow is fenced off for the exclusive use of a handful of visitors? If this meadow were once again open for everything from kite flying and picnicking to soccer and concerts, pressure on the Sheep Meadow would be reduced and its scarred turf given a chance to recover. Commissioner Heckscher, by having the fence removed from the southern playground, has most commendably led the way towards giving their precious open space back to the people of the city.

As you turn away from the man-made wasteland of North Meadow, return to the drinking fountain and pass to its left along the path bordering the north margin of the meadow. The slope to the left is dotted with a scattering of narrow pin oaks and unthrifty hybrid elms, a succession of unrelated bare trunks, barren of interest or repose. The view becomes increasingly bleak as you look up the slope. Here are a few high branched trees and a monotony of grass, all visible at a glance, holding no surprise from any viewpoint, and so utterly sterile and uninviting that there is no inducement to explore. This is precisely the see-through effect Olmsted wished to avoid when he ordered trees planted in "groups, passages, and masses of foliage. The native underwood is to be planted in thickets and allowed to grow in natural forms, enough of it being introduced to prevent a grove or orchard-like monotony of trunks."

Turn your back on this impoverished scene and look over the meadow to its far end. If you have a vigorous imagination, duplicate the great elm at the southwest corner and place its twin on the south margin where the lost elm stood in July. In your mind's eye, the tree's broad canopy nearly fills the blank segment of the sky and its shadow hides the path and all but a hint of the barrier planting along the transverse road. If you can visualize this noble tree as it commanded the view, you have recaptured the essence of Olmsted's pastoral scene:

> "The planting generally is designed to give the broadest effects of light and shade which can be obtained upon the ground, and to produce the impression of great space and freedom, while at the same time the visitor may keep in dense shade if he prefer it."

The word "broad" recurs as a dominant theme in Olmsted's writings and may be taken as the gauge by which all plantings must be considered before approval—as will be done when each of the Olmsted parks has a strong professional horticultural director.

Subject to such approval, I submit that it would be consistent with Olmsted's broad landscape to plant a grove of sweet gums to replace the lost elm at the south end of East Meadow. I've suggested plantings for the rocky hill to the west. The thin barrier along roads at south and west, and the paltry planting of the slope to the north of East Meadow could be given substance by the introduction of solid-foliaged, broad-branching trees: white, red, black, shingle, and Turkey oaks; beech; silver lindens; sweet gums; horsechestnuts and buckeyes; and the massive-headed *Magnolia acuminata* to be seen on Tour VIII. Under the sparse trees near the crown of the hill, irregular thickets of understory trees and shrubs would create Olmsted's "intricate disposition of lights and shadows sufficient to affect the imagination with a sense of mystery."

Returning from dream planting to the trees actually standing around East Meadow, let's walk forward to the two-trunked tree on the right, slightly beyond lamp post #9910. If you come on this walk in September, the flash of glossy red leaves will tell you at once that this is a sour gum, *Nyssa sylvatica*. Though a water-loving tree, this one seems to be making the best of a dry situation.

The sour gum has a variety of regional names: pep-peridge and tupelo in New England, black gum and bee gum in the South. The flowers are inconspicuous but are the source of a delicately flavored honey usually sold as tupelo honey. The bluish fruits are relished by song and game birds as well as by possums and bears. Wood of the sour gum is prone to decay, especially the heartwood, so hollow trees are common. When these are sawed into sections and roofed with boards, they are set up as bee hives and so give the tree its country name of bee gum.

It is a great misfortune that the sour gum is so intolerant of root disturbance. If it were easier to transplant, it could be used wherever its glorious early color is mirrored in water, or where it can stand ablaze in a sunny clearing at the edge of woods with still-green trees as backdrop.

As you pass the playground entrance, look in towards the Fifth Avenue side where a sweet gum stands between swings and sandbox. When you study its healthy, vigor-ous appearance, I believe you will share my admiration for this outstanding native and agree that it can scarcely be used too often.

If you come to East Meadow on a fair day around noon, you will see one of the prettiest sights in the park. During the lunch hour, the staff of Mount Sinai Hospital come out for refreshment, looking in their white and pale blue uniforms like a flock of doves on the grass. If any proof is needed of the magically healing effect of Olmsted and Vaux's pastoral landscape, it is provided by the busy young people who spend their working hours among the sick and injured and come into the park for a restoring breath of peace and health.

"The special value of the Central Park to the city of New York will lie, and even now lies, in its comparative largeness. There are certain kinds of beauty possible to be had in it which it is not possible for the city to have anywhere else, because on no other ground of the city is there scope and breadth enough for them. Such beauty as there is in a flower bed, such beauty as there is in a fir tree . . . can be had even in the back yard of a city house. Central Park can be better used. That which is expected to be especially valuable on the Central Park is the beauty of broad landscape scenes and of combinations of trees with trees and with rocks and turf and water.

No man is to use the discretion given him to secure pretty little local effects, at the expense of general effects and especially of broad landscape effects."

Frederick Law Olmsted, 1873

VI

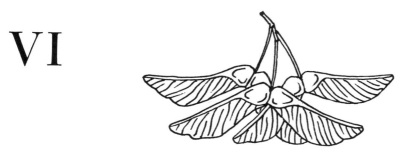

SHEEP MEADOW

72nd Street and Central Park West

On this tour we shall view the Sheep Meadow, renew our acquaintance with an English oak, and add a hop tree, silverbell, cork tree, and golden rain tree to our list.

As you face the park, take the footpath to the right of the road and walk under a rustic arbor covered with wisteria, a favorite spot for relaxing in dappled shade and a bower of fragrance in May when the wisteria is in bloom. On the left, beyond lamp post #7107, is a Norway maple which you will recognize by its smoothly lined bark, thin-textured leaves, and horizontal key fruits.

Next on the embankment at the left are two small twisted trees with three-part leaves. These are hop trees, *Ptelea trifoliata,* a rather uncommon native of our eastern coast. This is a patchwork tree put together in an off moment when nature ran out of invention and rummaged in her scrap basket for leftover designs. The leaves look alarmingly like those of poison ivy; the shining reddish-brown bark with rows of lenticels (breathing pores) might be taken for that of cherry; and the fruits—flat papery disks enclosing two seeds—are an enlarged replica of the elm's. The hop tree is not related to any of these proto-types but belongs to the rue family which includes citrus fruits, cork tree, and spiny ash. It has more value as a curiosity than as an ornament.

Sixty feet beyond lamp post #7105 on the right are two pin oaks, and beyond them, three Osage oranges, *Maclura pomifera.* The nearest and largest one, with a trunk dividing in two about 5 feet above ground, and the one behind it near the bridle path, are both females, as you can tell in late summer from their burden of char-treuse, grapefruit-sized fruit. Don't walk under the trees in November when the fruit starts to fall! It is hard and heavy enough to inflict a painful bruise.

The wood of Osage orange is exceptionally tough and pliant. It was prized by Indians and frontiersmen as the prime wood for making bows. One of its common names, Bodart, is a corruption of the French *bois d'arc,* or bow-wood.

Extracts of the roots and inner bark were used by Indians to dye their blanket yarns. This may seem remote in time but the use of Osage orange as a dyestuff was revived in this century. The making of aniline dyes had been almost exclusively a German industry. When World War I cut off the import of German dyes, Osage orange was used to color khaki uniforms.

The fruits of the Osage orange are called oranges in

94

the common name and apples in the scientific one. In fact they are neither: the tree belongs to the mulberry family. If you slice the fruit across, you'll find it much like a pineapple in texture: juicy and with radiating fibers but (unlike a pineapple) containing large seeds. The fruit is not palatable to human taste. Its acrid juice and the sap of the tree may cause skin irritation in sensitive individuals. However, it is relished by squirrels which are often seen carrying off chunks bigger than their head.

On the embankment to the left, stretching from the row of benches to lamp post #7101, is a sorry tangle of weed-choked garden shrubs, plants as unsuited to competing in the wild as cage-bred canaries. The one thriving shrub is the Eurasian *Viburnum opulus* with the more-than-ordinarily misleading name of Guelder rose. The leaves slightly resemble those of maple but are distinguished by little stemless glands on the leafstalk near the base of the leaf, as you can confirm with a hand lens. Foliage turns a splendid flame color in autumn and the fruits—translucent red like oversize currants—persist well into winter.

Walk ahead to the road and cross at the traffic light. On the far side, the first tree behind the benches at the right is a black oak, *Quercus velutina.* Broad shining leaves, nearly black bark broken into small rough plates, and heavy horizontal branches are the first points of recognition. To clinch the identity, look at the buds under your hand lens. If they are four-angled, dull brown, and matted with grayish hairs, you can be sure that you have a black oak. The acorn is enclosed for half its length in a bowl-shaped cup covered with coarse, protruding scales.

The next tree shows typical black oak buds but its leaves are small and deeply cut, probably indicating an admixture of pin oak blood.

Walk on farther into the park, passing a rock outcrop and a short path leading to the bowling greens. Just beyond this path is a young English oak, *Q. robur,* a gift of the Friends of Central Park. The leaves are at eye level so you can study them more easily than on the taller specimen seen towards the end of Tour II. Leaves are round lobed like those of our native white oak but are heavier in texture and much smaller, usually not over 4 inches in length. The leafstalk is so short that the leaf seems to grow directly from the twig. The unique hallmark of the English oak is its auricles, the little earlike ruffles that ornament the base of the leaf and sometimes meet over the short leafstalk. Given space to develop, the English oak becomes at maturity a truly noble tree with massive trunk and heavy low branches.

In the open space to the north of the footpath once stood the Mineral Springs Pavilion or Spa, designed by Calvert Vaux and built in 1868. It was a deliciously fanciful, highly colored building, well screened by trees so that its presence didn't detract from the pastoral atmosphere of the Sheep Meadow, then called the Green, a name that survives in Tavern-on-the-Green. The Spa was a city dweller's Saratoga Springs, with mineral water dispensed from bottles. The benefits of a visit to the Spa, attributed to the medicinal properties of the waters, were quite as likely due to the stimulation of a walk in the fresh air. The building, like other architectural treasures in the park, fell into disrepair through lack of maintenance. It was torn down in 1960.

For a jarring example of the decline of aesthetic standards in this self-proclaimed Age of Culture, look ahead to the new concession building, a triumph of commercialism over taste. A stark, squat mass of glaring red brick, it was deliberately designed and sited to dominate the landscape like a fort.

Olmsted and Vaux were humanitarians with deep psychological insight. They planned Central Park as a haven of mental and physical refreshment, a refuge from the rigid geometry of the future city. Spacious tree-bordered

96

meadows, while beautiful in themselves, had a deeper therapeutic purpose: to provide, as Olmsted wrote, "a feeling of relief on escaping from the cramped, confined, and controlling circumstances of the streets of the town; in other words, *a sense of enlarged freedom. . . .*" Olmsted's use of italics stresses the crucial importance he gave to this concept. The phrase, and the noble breadth of vision it embodies, should be the touchstone that tests all policies affecting Central Park.

In 1858 when Olmsted and Vaux entered the competition for a design for Central Park, they signed their entry "Greensward" because, as Olmsted wrote, "it presented larger unbroken surfaces of turf and of water than any other." Of the five major expanses of greensward, only East Meadow and the Sheep Meadow remain open for multiple use—which means, inevitably, overuse. No turf can endure the assault of millions of feet in all seasons and all weathers, even when the ground is spongy with rain or melting frost. If North Meadow were again made available for use by all park visitors, it would draw off some of the crowds that now trample the Sheep Meadow to dust or mud.

The very fact of overuse demonstrates how vital the park's unimpeded open spaces are to the life of the city. Except for the glowering concession building and a snaggle of asphalt paths, the Sheep Meadow has escaped major encroachment. It is a stupendous achievement that the New York Philharmonic concerts, the park's most illustrious cultural activity, are performed on the Sheep Meadow with no permanent structure to deface the landscape and at no charge to the public. The dazzling concept of a bandshell on wheels originated with the Philharmonic. The shell was purchased by the City of New York and named in honor of Mrs. Charles S. Guggenheimer whose Stadium Concerts were an innovative gift of fine music to the people. Equal praise is due the third

97

partner, the Jos. Schlitz Brewing Company, for helping defray the annual cost of the concerts without advertising signs or commercial ballyhoo. The whole complex enterprise is carried off with such taste, dedication, and respect for the park that it serves as a model for the use of public land. The concerts bring joy and enrichment to millions. When the music is ended and the vans pull away, the Sheep Meadow returns to its pastoral state.

The Sheep Meadow may have escaped structural invasion but it has not been so lucky with its planting. As you face the meadow, let your glance drift around its margin. It will jump from one naked tree trunk to another like a stick rattled along a picket fence. There is no area of repose on which the eye can linger.

Olmsted's directions for planting the borders of large meadows are detailed and comprehensive.

> "The North Meadow, the green and the Play ground, except where large rocks prevent, are to be bordered by scattered trees, singly and in small clusters or loose groups, all of kinds which will grow large and spread widely; that is to say with characteristic park trees. They are to be formed with low heads but not so low that sheep cannot graze under them. Trees on these grounds which have been trimmed to long naked trunks are to be shortened in to force new lower branching."

East Meadow, as we have just seen, was designed in accordance with these principles. Where the original planting survives, the effect is tranquil and satisfying. By contrast, on the borders of the Sheep Meadow, wide-spreading trees have been replaced by narrow, thin-foliaged pin oaks and hybrid elms, all limbed up like telephone poles. Dense-headed trees such as were recommended to fill the thin spots in East Meadow's border are imperatively needed here.

A first step towards redeeming the Sheep Meadow would be elimination of the unused roadway on its east

98

margin. If this land were restored to the park and heavily planted, it would materially strengthen the puny, see-through border.

Screens of tall trees, often given additional height by being planted on a ridge, were Olmsted's device for blocking out "the artificial wall, twice as high as the Great Wall of China, composed of urban buildings. Whenever this should appear across a meadow-view, the imagination would be checked abruptly at short range." Even with his uncanny foresight, Olmsted could hardly have envisioned the Great Wall that would result from a scarcely-noted event of 1857: the installation by Elisha Groves Otis of a vertical railway for lifting passengers in a New York City department store.

The towering city buildings can't be ignored. They might, however, be less overwhelming if the planting of the park at their feet held some compelling interest—a luxuriance of broad-headed trees with varied foliage textures, and masses of flowering shrubs and vines to clothe barren mounds of rock with color and fragrance.

Let's walk back behind the concession building again, and take the first right turn after lamp post #6847. As you walk past the glacier-scarred outcrops, you must imagine them dressed with creeping shrubs, mosses, and flowering alpine plants as they were before the Tweed Ring and its obtuse park commissioners set about "improving" Olmsted's masterpiece to suit their own vulgar tastes. In his *Spoils of the Park,* Olmsted writes with bitterness distilled from long frustration:

> "Rocky passages of the Park, which had been furnished under my direction with a natural growth of rocky hillside perennials, have been more than once 'cleaned up,' and so thoroughly that the leaf-mould, with which the crevices of the ledge had been carefully filled for the sustenance of the plants, was swept out with house-brooms. . . . The work is still going on, I am assured, at this moment (1882); and when

it is finished, and August comes round again, and all the yellow turf and the dead, half-covered outcrops of smooth-faced, gray and brown ledge are fully exposed to view, God help the poor man who can find no better place of escape from the town!"

Many of the rock plants Olmsted used to simulate a verdant alpine meadow are too fragile for a park without guards or any public discipline. There are plenty of rugged plants, however, to drape the barren rocks that Olmsted deplored. Creeping junipers form low billowing mats of silver-green, sea green, or misty blue prickly foliage. Fragrant sumach, *Rhus aromatica,* is a vigorous, wide spreading, semi-prostrate native. Its shining three-part leaves turn an incandescent red in autumn, making a stunning mass of color for crevice or shelf. The red-berried *Cotoneaster horizontalis,* as its common name of rock spray indicates, is a large scale garnish that spreads its broad fans to root in any available crevice.

Olmsted's sympathetic partnership with nature has in many cases triumphed over attempts by small-minded caretakers to reduce a varied and picturesque landscape to "the uniformly smug and smart suburban door-yard style." An instance is the dramatic struggle of a two-trunked elm on the right, opposite lamp post #7013, as its roots clasp the rock to keep from toppling off the cliff. The tree can't have been deliberately planted in such a narrow crevice but must have sprung from wind-blown seed. This is one of the felicitous accidents that Olmsted anticipated when he asked critics not to judge Central Park for forty years, when nature had added her bounty to man's handiwork.

At the far end of the outcrop, a small hackberry has found a foothold in its chosen site, a hairline fault in the rock. Hackberries are one of the commonest self-sown native trees in Central Park as they thrive on its austere cliffs and rock-underlaid soil. By contrast, hackberries do

100

poorly in Prospect Park's deep, open soil, where they tend to yellowed leaves, lanky growth, and a sparse crop of undersized witches' brooms.

As you approach the end of the footpath, try your skill at identifying the oaks on the left. Their bark is lined with pale gray, vertical ribbons. The medium-sized leaves with bristle-tipped lobes and red-tinged leafstalks are additional clues. For positive identification, examine the buds under a hand lens. If they are chestnut brown, shining, and hairless except for the tips of the scales, you can check off a red oak with assurance.

When you reach the main path at the foot of the hill, turn right and walk to the traffic light. Cross the road and on the far side, turn right on the footpath and walk up the hill until you come to a black-painted wooden sign on the left. (It says "Horse-shoe Parking," if you want to walk around to the front to confirm your position.) The three-trunked tree directly behind the sign is a silverbell, *Halesia carolina,* one of the treasures of our southern highlands. In early spring, the lush valleys of the Great Smokies are a bower of silverbell, dogwood, and redbud over a pink and white carpet of spring beauties. The silverbell's off-white flowers, hung profusely from every leaf axil, are followed by inflated pods with four wings down the sides.

Just to the left of the silverbell is one of the cryptic, non-fruiting hornbeams, an exceptionally well-shaped tree with broad branches sweeping to the ground. Even with the help of a mounted policeman, whose higher viewpoint allowed him to survey the upper branches, not a single fruit cluster could be seen. The tiny buds and delicate twigs point to the American hornbeam, *Carpinus caroliniana.* Another distinction, though a rather superficial one, is that European hornbeams show no marked autumn color while the American puts on a modest show of yellow and red. If you study the tree for the first time

101

in October, jot down your observation of foliage color as a preliminary check, subject to confirmation when it produces fruit. If it is indeed an American, then it is an uncommonly vigorous and flourishing specimen of this usually frail-looking tree. It merits a dressing of leafmold over its roots to keep it in top condition.

Now return to the Horse-shoe Parking sign, turn sharp left around it, and walk up the road to lamp post #7100. Twenty-five feet up the slope behind the lamp post is a tree with pinnately compound leaves on opposite branches. If you turn back to the key on page 11, you'll find two trees that fit this category: the ashes and cork tree. If you find that the winter buds are concealed by the conical base of the leafstalk, you can be sure that this is a cork tree. The undersides of the leaves, thickly matted with fine white hairs, identify it as *Phellodendron amurense* var. *lavallei*, by far the commonest variety in the park. This is presumably a male tree as it had no fruit.

Follow the road up to the fountain in the center of the Carriage Concourse. Cars still nose up to the basin where horses once drank but the fountain is long since dry. If it could be put into operation again as an ornament, it would help redeem this sterile expanse of asphalt.

Cross the Concourse to the northwest, aiming for the temple-topped towers of the San Remo. In the angle of the path that leads down to the Lake is a cut-leaf beech, a variety of the European beech, *Fagus sylvatica*. You may recall seeing a sorry specimen, crowded and shaded, near the end of Tour II. This one, better situated in sun, shows to advantage its ferny foliage, richly colored, clean, and full. It is recorded in Peet as part of the original planting.

When allowed to grow naturally, a cut-leaf beech branches nearly to the ground. Its dense growth makes an impenetrable thicket, protecting the root area from compaction while its shade keeps the soil cool and moist.

This specimen has been limbed up as if it were a street tree. Both its trunk and roots have suffered from exposure.

As you walk south, perhaps 40 feet beyond lamp post #7104, you will pass a curving flight of rough stone steps. These led to a boat landing beneath a rustic shelter. If you step out onto the rock ledge, you can see the base of the shelter to the left of the point. On the point, a magnificent Turkey oak clasps the rocky shore with its serpentine roots. It is being crowded by a badly placed willow which diminishes the dramatic solitude of the oak. The oak was planted by Olmsted's plan; the intruding willow was added by a lesser hand. If in imagination you can blot out the willow and replace it with a mass of low bushes to soften the blank shore on the left, you will see how the oak at once assumes its intended dominance— and even more clearly, recognize the need to have all planting supervised by a sensitive landscape architect.

Before you leave the Lake, notice once again the skilled use of existing rocks and the way the terminus of the Lake is concealed as it curves behind a well-shrubbed bend. Two densely planted groves of bald cypress once stood at the extreme tip of the little cove and on its far bank to the left. Their soaring columnar trunks must have made an impressive backdrop when seen from this point or from a boat coming down the Lake towards the landing. The present thinned planting betrays the illusion of natural scenery by permitting automobiles to be seen. In addition to bald cypresses, the misplaced willow could well be moved here, with a thick barrier planting of shrubs beneath.

South of the ledge are three unhappy hemlocks, *Tsuga canadensis.* These trees of cool woodlands are not likely to survive on this sun-baked rock. A number of sassafras saplings find the site congenial and are spreading into a thicket. Their green, powdered twigs are a key to identity in or out of leaf.

103

Between the sassafras and a large Norway maple, look down the slope towards the Lake. If it is early autumn, you will see a family of sour gums with their glorious color duplicated by reflection in the water.

Fifteen feet beyond the Norway maple, a small tree, only about 5 inches in diameter, leans out over the path to get light. This is a cork tree, again the common hairy-leafed variety, but this time a female tree. In October it bears large clusters of pea-sized fruit, so attractive to birds that any naturalist can overlook the slippery mess the crushed berries make on the sidewalk. Uneaten berries dry like raisins and remain on the trees to provide emergency rations for the first returning migrants of spring.

As you make a right turn onto the main walk that borders the roadway, notice the good thick stand of *Cornus mas* in the angle of the path. You will know it at once in late March by its small mustard-yellow flowers and in autumn by its rose-red foliage. Between seasons, check the vein pattern and buds as described on page 108.

Walk towards Daniel Webster as he stands frowning at the lingerie ruffle of petunias at his feet. Olmsted warned against an influx of statues because they invite petty details. The Commissioners of the Park attempted to bar memorials to the dead, however worthy, from a pleasure ground where people come "to dispel thoughts of business and memories calculated to sadden or oppress." Samuel Parsons, Jr., the valiant defender of Central Park whose work we shall see on the next tour, spoke with a landscape architect's understanding of "the soft, mellow, enticing charm" of a naturalistic park. He added a penetrating analysis: "Mystery is one of the greatest values in this kind of landscape gardening, and the more definite lines of sculpture must necessarily tend to dissipate the appearance of mystery."

In this as in other park matters, crude bureaucrats and

aggressive philanthropists overcame the counsel of good taste. Of the statues that were forced on Central Park, Webster's is by no means the worst. Where statues have invaded the park, they might be given stability by underplanting with evergreens, not window-box annuals. Clipped yews, Japanese hollies, hemlock, or juniper would relate in scale and permanence to the bronze and granite intrusion.

The shortest way to 72nd Street and Central Park West is up the slight hill across the road. Halfway up you will pass a black cherry leaning over the path at the right, then a flattish rock. Diagonally opposite on the left is a taller tree with an untreated wound on the trunk. This is a river birch, *Betula nigra,* a highly desirable and insufficiently used subject with gracefully dipping branches. It is one of the intermediate trees that would help to restore the luxuriant understory planting along watersides. Despite its scientific name, the bark is not black but yellowish, sometimes with tinges of red. The leaf is wedge shaped, without teeth on the basal margin, then doubly toothed on the tapering outer edges.

The pine on the right is an Austrian pine, *Pinus nigra,* the most frequently seen evergreen conifer in the park because it is one of the very few that can tolerate polluted city air. The bark shows conspicuous raised plates of gray or tan, separated by dark brown or reddish brown crevices. Needles are two to a bundle, up to 6 inches long, and twisted in a way that gives the tree a somewhat frowsty, uncombed look. With age, the drooping branches create a wonderfully picturesque effect. When seen against the sky, they recall the hilltop pines in Japanese prints and Chinese brush-drawn landscapes.

As you come to the road, cross by the tumbledown wisteria arbor and walk almost to lamp post #7200. A few feet behind the row of benches on the right is a golden rain tree, *Koelreuteria paniculata,* one of the scarce and prized summer-flowering trees. The koelreuteria is distinguished by its pinnately compound leaves with leaflets sometimes opposite, sometimes alternate, but always deeply toothed or even slashed on the margins. If you'll think back, you'll find that all the other pinnately compound leaves we've seen—those of ailanthus, hickory, ash, sumach, cork tree, locust, sophora—have leaflets with nearly smooth margins, so the jagged edges of koelreuteria leaflets are an instant key to identity.

In mid-July the koelreuteria puts on a brief but showy display of small, chrome yellow flowers in wide-spreading clusters as much as 18 inches long and nearly as wide. Flowers are followed by persistent balloonlike capsules, at first light green, then ripening to bright yellow-brown. These make a striking contrast against the deep green foliage and look as festive as strings of miniature Chinese lanterns at a late summer garden party.

"Your majesty should commit your favorite horses to the care of an ignorant groom, or place your choice cattle in charge of an ignorant cow-boy, rather than entrust your trees and shrubs to the manipulation of an ignorant gardener. But, above all the candidates for the supervision of your park, *beware of petty politicians.*"

Linnaeus to Gustavus III of Sweden.

VII

RHODODENDRON MILE

*85th Street and
Fifth Avenue*

Tᴴɪs very short walk provides an opportunity to compare a Norway and a sycamore maple growing side by side, to learn the distinction between two superficially similar shrubs, and to add a black walnut to your tree list.

Enter the park just north of 85th Street. On the left of the path is a stretch of the native black haw, *Viburnum prunifolium*, scrawny specimens limbed up so high that all their fountainy grace is destroyed. If you remember the properly grown, low-arching black haws you saw in the Ramble (page 67) you may also recall their bark pat-

107

tern of small lizard-skin plates, very much like that of the flowering dogwood. Other points of similarity between viburnum and dogwood are the opposite branching pattern and beautiful rose-red autumn color. However, a study of the leaves, buds, and fruit will establish the differences. Let's start first with the viburnum because it is nearest and then move on to a shrubby dogwood, *Cornus mas*, alongside the steps.

You may not be able to memorize all the keys but if you check them off one by one, the salient points will stick in your mind. Leaf margins of the viburnum are toothed, so finely that you may need a hand lens to make them out. The secondary veins extend at an acute angle and almost in a straight line to the margin. Leafstalks are often winged, that is, the base of the leaf is prolonged in a narrow ribbon along each side of the stalk. Flower buds are dull brown, slender, and pointed, as much as ½ inch long, and usually produced at the tips of the shoots. The fruit is oval and delicately colored, at first ivory with a pink flush, then ripening very late in the season to blue-black. If you come upon the viburnum in May, you will of course distinguish its flat-topped clusters of small white flowers from the yellow-flowered *Cornus mas*.

While details are fresh in mind, make a sharp turn to the right at #9500 and go partway up the steps between generous masses of the dogwood. You'll note that these favored shrubs are allowed to form a low-branched tangle, as dense a thicket as you'll find anywhere in the park. If this luxuriant growth doesn't constitute a threat to public safety, then why in the name of consistency are the viburnums mutilated, along with most of the park's shrubs?

Remembering the toothed leaves of the viburnum, notice that the leaves of the dogwood are smooth edged, and that the veins bend to follow the curve of the margin almost to the tip. Buds are small, roundish, light yellow-

108

tan, and often borne in the axils of paired leaves or twigs. The fruit is large and olive-shaped, clear scarlet, ripening in August, and quickly stripped by birds. Again the flowers are distinctive: a profusion of tiny mustard-yellow tufts cover the naked branches in late March or early April.

Turn around now and look down the steps to your left to a European hornbeam, *Carpinus betulus,* the largest yet found in Central Park. Even though injured by drought and snow, it is a beautifully formed tree, unusually tall and highly decorative when its branches droop under the weight of its fruit clusters. Because of its exceptional quality and prominent position, this hornbeam was one of the ten selected for treatment through the Camperdown Fund in 1969.

The topmost branches, broken in the February 1969 snowstorm, hung over the tree like a half-open umbrella. When these were cut away, a large amount of long-dead wood was revealed. With all dead and splintered wood removed, as well as sucker growth from the lower branches, the leafless frame of the tree looks a bit sparse. It was given a generous feeding to promote new root development and this in turn, it is hoped, will stimulate growth in the newly cleared top. In tree as in human surgery, there is no guarantee: the doctor does his best to repair an injury but actual healing rests with the patient.

Treatment of the hornbeam was made possible by a gift to the Camperdown Fund from a nearby resident who is actively concerned with the welfare of the park. To make the tree's recovery doubly sure, the donor intends to provide shrubs to curb trampling over its root area. With so much good will and effort expended in its behalf, the tree is virtually obligated to show immediate improvement.

Turn again as if to climb the stairs but look to the slope

on your left where a poplar leans towards the path. Like the specimen seen near the end of Tour IV (page 76) this is one of a series of hybrids between our native cottonwood, *Populus deltoides*, and the European black poplar, *P. nigra*, a species best known for its fastigiate form, the Lombardy poplar. These hybrids originated in France about 1750 at a time when the astonishing wealth of North American plant material was creating a sensation on the Continent. The group name, *Populus* x *canadensis*, suggests that the northern form of cottonwood was shipped to France, perhaps from Quebec, where it crossed by accident or plan with the European species.

All the poplars I have examined in Central Park belong to this group of hybrids, or "swarm" as it is called by botanists. The term refers to an assortment of individuals arising from multiple crossing of the same parent species, and exhibiting as many variations as members of a human family. For example, in this specimen, the flat (deltoid) base of the leaf and its long tapering tip point to *P. deltoides*; the fine teeth and absence of basal glands are characteristic of *nigra*. In the poplar we saw by the Lake, the wedge-shaped base and absence of glands are typical of *nigra* while the large incurved teeth and fat sticky buds are marks of *deltoides*. Hybrids present pitfalls for the innocent amateur who tries to establish identification by matching leaf shapes to pictures in a book. To start with, you have to know that *deltoides* has glands at the base of the leaf in order to notice that they are missing! It takes the distillation of a whole library and the intensive, diversified knowledge of a lifetime of study to spot the discrepancies, and here once more I am indebted to George Kalmbacher for steering me away from a novice's blunder.

Now climb the stairs and turn sharp left at the top. Just beyond a rectangular jog in the fence is a lordly tree, a black walnut, *Juglans nigra*. The deeply ridged bark is a beautiful deep, rich reddish brown. The pinnately compound leaves have a distinctive oddity: very often the terminal leaflet is missing and the leaf ends in a pair of leaflets like rabbit ears.

Black walnut wood was a favorite of cabinetmakers because of its fine grain and resistance to warping. Excessive demand caused its extermination in some regions, and a tree of this size would be hard to find in the wild. The sweet, oily nutmeats are hard to extract from the convoluted shells but those who enjoy their unique flavor in cookies and confections think the effort is well spent.

The pigmentation of walnuts is potent and durable. Husks of the butternut, *Juglans cinerea,* yield a tan dye which was used to color a coarse homespun cloth suitable for trousers or overalls. The color was so distinctive that its name became a derisive slang term: backwoods soldiers of the Confederacy were known as Butternuts. Similarly, green husks of the black walnut, chopped up and steeped in water, produce a beautiful and lasting dye ranging in depth from rich brown to black. In English stories, any child preparing to run away to join the gypsies first stained hands and face with walnut juice.

Another black walnut stands beyond the last bench on the lower path. It is a smaller tree with branches low enough so that you can study the leaves at close range.

As you pass the end of the fenced triangle, the first large tree on the left, 20 feet down the slope, is a Norway maple, *Acer platanoides.* Just beyond it to the right, 12 feet from the path, is a sycamore maple, *Acer pseudoplatanus.* (Both names indicate a resemblance to a plane tree, *Platanus.*) This is the first time we have seen them growing close enough for immediate comparison.

The Norway maple has finely grooved, tight fitting bark, paper-thin leaves, and key fruits horizontally aligned like an aviator's insignia. Chartreuse flowers are borne in rounded clusters on naked branches in late April.

Turning to the sycamore maple, you will notice that the

111

bark is scaly and, on mature trunks, could be peeled in roundish flakes. Leaves are thick textured with prominent veins on the underside. Their leafstalks are often tinged with red. Yellow-green flowers dangle in long clusters below the branches in May after leaves are fully developed. Flowers are followed by chains of key fruits whose wings meet at a sharp angle, sometimes with their inner tips touching. As these chains hang on the tree long after the leaves have fallen, the sycamore maple can be instantly recognized even at a distance.

Beyond this pair, the two maples are repeated in the same order, growing so close together that their branches touch. All details of leaf, flower, and fruit can be compared and fixed permanently in memory. The sycamore maple is too young to show the bark pattern found on mature trees.

At the end of the fence, 25 feet down the slope, is a bald cypress, *Taxodium distichum*. A sun-baked south-facing slope is hardly the best site for a tree of the swamp-lands: it shows the effect of hardship in its spare outline.

The finest bald cypresses in the park are on the east border of Harlem Meer above 106th Street. Their towering trunks and delicate fernlike foliage make an unforgettable impression when seen across the water.

Early pictures show that Olmsted and Vaux used Lombardy poplars as vertical accents on the Lake shore, notably to point up boat landings and on the bank at the north end of Bow Bridge. These brittle, borer-ridden trees have long since disappeared. An even more dramatic effect could be achieved by planting long-lived bald cypresses where the poplars once stood.

The bald cypress is one of the very few needle-leafed trees that shows a color change in autumn. Its needles turn amber and orange, a pleasing complement to the cinnamon-colored bark, before they fall. The true larches show muted yellow and brown tones. The golden larch

112

which we'll see on the last tour earns its common name by a striking display of green gold and tawny orange, set off by a profusion of large, light green cones.

The most spectacular of the deciduous conifers (non-evergreen cone-bearers) is the metasequoia, *M. glyptostroboides*, which resembles the bald cypress but excels it in every way. Long known only in fossil form and believed extinct, the metasequoia was found growing in China in 1946. It is surely the most exciting plant introduction of the century and should be available for study in Central Park. It is a rugged, fast growing tree with deep orange bark and fine, dark green needles which turn a glowing coppery fawn color in autumn. The straight, channeled trunk, expanding at the base and extended by buttress roots, has a strong architectural quality. I have a dream that when the scruffy, irregular hybrid elms on the Mall are eliminated, they might be replaced with ranks of metasequoias. These rather narrow-headed trees can never achieve the cathedral roof of the original American elms, but their stately columnar trunks would equal and perhaps surpass the formal aisles of elm boles. My dream looks forward to the day when our historic urban parks will be put beyond the reach of politics and governed by the country's most eminent horticulturists and historical landscape architects, men of unimpeachable qualification and integrity such as those who administer the National Trust gardens in Great Britain.

To come down to earth with a thud, walk ahead to a clearing where a gift of garden shrubs—mock orange, forsythia, and lilac among others—was planted on a slope infested with polygonum. In housekeeping terms, this is equivalent to putting down costly broadloom on a floor undermined by termites.

The polygonum should have been thoroughly killed by repeated sprayings with a powerful herbicide before any planting was done. Now that the shrubs are in place,

113

spraying is no longer possible as the toxic agent will kill any plant it touches. Instead, it will be necessary to eliminate the weed shoot by shoot with poison hand-applied with a paintbrush. This is best done in early spring when the soft red noses of the polygonum first push through the ground. If these shoots are conscientiously dabbed with herbicide as fast as they appear, perhaps twice a week, the planting may be saved. As is usually the case, correcting a slovenly piece of work is far more tedious and exacting than doing a workmanlike job of preparation at the outset.

In May when rhododendrons are in flower, you'll want to choose a no-car day to stroll north on East Drive to admire the border on the reservoir side.

The Sage Plantation, or Rhododendron Mile as it was popularly called, was established in 1908 and rapidly gained fame throughout the world. It was the product of a touching partnership between Mrs. Russell Sage, a gentle philanthropist of advanced years, and Samuel Parsons, Jr., then Landscape Architect of Central Park. Mrs. Sage, after the death of her husband, quietly set about to beautify the city through her immense fortune. Her husband had enjoyed a daily drive through the park, as did Mrs. Sage; she often walked in the northern portion, where a devoted old park keeper reserved a rustic seat for her use. Adding beauty to her cherished park was a natural outlet for Mrs. Sage's bounty. She wished to give far more: she offered nearly a million dollars on condition that Parsons should execute the work. The park commissioner of the day, jealous of Parsons' great prestige, refused the gift on Mrs. Sage's terms.

In Samuel Parsons, Mrs. Sage found the perfect instrument to carry out her wishes. Literally a born plantsman, he was the grandson of the founder of Parsons' Nursery, established in 1840 and now part of Kissena

Park in Queens. In the nursery, the young man received priceless practical training before going on to Sheffield Scientific School at Yale. His long and honored association with the park began in 1882 as Calvert Vaux's Superintendent of Planting, and continued from Landscape Architect to Park Commissioner before retirement in 1911. He was known as "The Last of the Incorruptibles" for his uncompromising stand against political interference and the unceasing threat of encroachments and perversions of the Olmsted and Vaux ideal.

The Sage Plantation was Parsons' brilliant solution to the handling of a long, narrow strip of land. About 7000 rhododendrons, chosen for clarity and range of color, hardiness, and habit of growth, were purchased in England and Holland. As Parsons was a thoroughly competent plantsman, he devoted $20,000 of the $50,000 gift to preparing the soil, improving its texture and fertility with loam and humus brought by barge from New Jersey.

Parsons gave careful instructions for watering and mulching the shrubs and for protecting them with evergreen boughs in winter, but after his retirement, the level of care declined. Parsons wrote in his late years:

> "Neglect of the Sage rhododendrons came about, I am sorry to say, in a distinctly discreditable way. Ignorance and indifference probably caused the neglect. Perhaps the day will come when the Park Department, as it should in all decency, will replace the dead portion of the kind old lady's gift to Central Park which she loved so well."

Rhododendron Mile was in fact replanted in 1969, in part through a substantial gift to the Friends of Central Park from donors who wish to remain anonymous. Mrs. Sage told her friends that the rhododendrons had given

115

her more pleasure than any other of her benefactions. This pleasure can once more be shared by park visitors as a double tribute to Mrs. Sage's enlightened philanthropy and to Samuel Parsons as staunch defender of the park they both loved and served.

"No park should in any way assume the office of a museum. Every tree or shrub employed in a park should find place there only as it shows value in the whole unified artistic effect. The fact that any plant has botanic interest should weigh not at all in its artistic employment. It is the hue and shape in the picture, the line in the horizon that we should always seek."

Samuel Parsons, Jr.

116

VIII

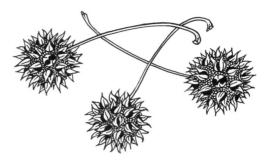

THE HEART OF
THE RAMBLE

Boat House: 74th Street near Fifth Avenue

THIS tour is an emotional roller coaster, swinging abruptly from rapture to rage. People with volatile blood pressure are advised to take suitable precautions. Two gigantic cork trees, Kentucky coffee trees, a monumental magnolia, and a *Styrax japonica* are some of the high spots. To see the styrax in bloom, time your visit for Memorial Day. The woods are enticing in all seasons but be sure to plan a tour in late October to enjoy the autumn foliage, especially colorful along the banks of the Gill.

117

The tour begins at the Boat House near 72nd Street, reached from either Fifth Avenue or Central Park West. It ends in the Ramble from which you may return to civilization by going downhill in any direction.

The starting point is the southeast corner of the Boat House in line with the footpath leading between the traffic light and lamp post #E7401 on the west side of East Drive. To help you get your bearings, look for a willow oak, *Quercus phellos,* in the angle between building and iron railing. The willow oak has narrow, toothless leaves, bristle-tipped when young. The willows you will see in the park all have toothed leaves, as you can readily confirm by examining the immense specimen at the southwest corner of the Boat House.

The willow oak has long been regarded as doubtfully hardy in the North—and with some justification, as its chief natural concentration is in the Gulf States, with an ever-narrowing ribbon of occurrence stretching northward along the coastal plains as far as Staten Island. Now that its hardiness has been established, the willow oak has begun to achieve the popularity it deserves. Its sun-dappled shadow makes it ideal for lawn planting and as a nurse tree for shade-loving shrubs such as rhododendrons.

Olmsted and Vaux, in their unending search for rarities, seem to have pioneered in the use of willow oaks. A specimen dating from the original planting and measuring 8¼ feet in circumference was seen near the start of Tour II. An even more extraordinary example with a girth of 10¼ feet stands in Prospect Park east of the Vale of Cashmere. This is one of ten giant trees given remedial pruning and wound treatment by the Bartlett Tree Company in the Friends of Prospect Park's third annual tree salvage program in 1969.

Four feet in from the fence corner is a little tree of exceptional merit and all-season interest. It is *Oxyden-*

drum arboreum, called sourwood, sorrel tree, and lily-of-the-valley tree. The last name refers to the showy, pendent clusters of white flowers produced in late June and early July. The flowers are not open lily-of-the-valley bells but are tight-lipped urns like those of blueberry, pieris, leucothoe, and heather—all members, with oxydendrum, of the large, varied, and invaluable heath family. Oxydendrum is unique in being the only full-sized tree of the heath family that is hardy in the North.

Upturned seed capsules, pale green or tan in color, follow the flowers and remain on the tree for months. Foliage turns a glorious saturated scarlet or mahogany red in October. Against the rich deep tones of the leaves, the drooping sprays of light-colored fruit stand out so conspicuously that they look like a second flowering.

Don't judge the quality of oxydendrums by this unhappy specimen. Oxydendrums are woodland trees, growing best in deep, porous, humus-rich soil. The merest smattering of ecology would rule out a parched site where the soil is packed by trampling feet. This specimen is offered for identification only because its position is easily charted. We'll see better examples in the Ramble where guideposts are few. If you learn oxydendrum characteristics from this tree, you will be able to spot the others even when they stand in a thicket of mixed growth.

Start walking up the hill, passing a pair of willow oaks in front of the Boat House and others on the median strip of the parking lot on the right. At the right of the walk near the end of the fence, and to the left on either side of lamp post #7526, are red maples, *Acer rubrum.* You will recall seeing them first on the shore of the Pool, and should remember their small, paper-thin leaves with three main lobes, shallow sinuses, and gray-green undersides. The bark of young trunks is as smooth and pale gray as that of beeches.

Red maples have two seasons of beauty: in late March

when red flowers on naked branches bring news of the return of life to the frozen earth, and in late October and early November when the foliage puts on a spectacular show of varied color. At first just the tips of scattered branches burn yellow, orange, and red against the still-green mass of the crown, then the dazzling colors spread until the whole tree is a conflagration.

Do you remember in kindergarten how you traced maple leaves, then dampened the paper and splashed on red, yellow, and green paint? No matter how variously the colors run and mingle, designs created with paint and paper are outstripped in brilliance by the pigments of the living leaf.

Continue up the hill, passing on the right a grove of hackberries whose broken branches record the disastrous snowstorm of February 1969. When you come to a Y fork with lamp post #7530 in its point, take the right-hand path to the top of the hill where a rock outcrop on the right lies across the path from #7622. Beyond the rock and along the path ahead on the right is a grove of Kentucky coffee trees, *Gymnocladus dioicus.* The three-foot leaves of this tree are doubly compound, that is, the main stalk is set with secondary stalks which in turn bear the leaflets.

In Central Park you'll find only two other trees that consistently produce doubly compound leaves. Both are seen near the start of Tour IX. One is *Aralia elata,* with toothed leaflets and such an array of prickles that you could never mistake it for the bland coffee tree. The other is *Albizzia julibrissin* var. *rosea,* which has drooping, pithy branches and soft fernlike foliage. The coffee tree has clusters of whitish flowers in May, quite large in the female, but not so conspicuous as the rose-pink shaving brush flowers of the albizzia in July. It is interesting that both coffee tree and albizzia belong to the pea family yet neither has the wing-and-keel flower so familiar in sweet pea, wisteria, and black locust.

The name *Gymnocladus* means "naked branch" and refers to the late leafing and early leaf fall that keep the tree bare for half the year. *Dioicus* is a variant of "dioecious," meaning separately sexed. Only female trees bear fruit. These are broad, thick, leathery pods containing large seeds. Homesteaders in the Middle South roasted the seeds and brewed them to make a substitute for coffee. According to report, the flavor was singularly nasty. The local product was set aside without regret when genuine coffee became available.

The last coffee tree in this group, just this side of a thicket of *Cornus mas,* is a female. You can see the big pods dangling under the branches well into winter, and if you scuffle in the fallen leaves beneath the tree, you may find a trophy to take home.

Continue walking around the curve to the right, passing London planes and more coffee trees, and stop at lamp post #7626 just this side of the first bench. Standing alone about 50 feet behind the bench is a stout-trunked tree with large leaves: *Magnolia acuminata,* called cucumber tree from the appearance of its unripe fruit. The flowers are large, floppy, short-lived, and—because of their greenish color—easily overlooked. This is a magnificent specimen of a native species too seldom planted in Central Park: a dense-headed tree, massive without being coarse, exactly the type that is needed to give weight to flimsy elm-and-pin-oak borders such as those around the Sheep Meadow and the north margin of East Meadow. One of the tree's most beautiful and easily recognized features is its bark: a mottled coppery color which, when seen in the warm light just before sunset, can take on near-pink tones.

This tree is shown in Peet and may be assumed to date from the original planting. Certainly its girth of 9¼ feet

121

at breast height attests to great age. At one time it was valued highly enough to be given skilled care. On the north side you will see fillings at the base, now nearly healed over. The decline of professional competence in the Park Department's gardening staff is reflected in an unpainted cut on the trunk, starting to decay, and a ragged hollow in the branch pointing to the benches. Because of the noble size of this tree, its picturesque branch pattern, and the scarcity of its kind in the park, I put it on the list of trees to be treated in 1969.

By the time Carl Lundborg, vice-president of the Bartlett Company, toured the park to check on my selections, the leaves had fallen and the full extent of havoc revealed. The main leader had apparently been struck by lightning many years ago. The shattered crown, untreated, rotted back to form a cavity, leaving the huge limbs supported only by a shell. Many limbs are hollow as a result of faulty pruning or none at all.

I walked round and round the tree looking for some encouraging sign to justify work on it. Without a sound trunk to serve as mooring, it would obviously be impossible to support the threatened limbs with cables. In the end, with the utmost reluctance, I was forced to bow to Mr. Lundborg's judgment that years of neglect had left the tree beyond hope of salvage. Much as I regret writing off this magnificent tree, I have to concede that it would be a better investment to buy the largest *Magnolia acuminata* that can safely be moved, and plant it in the meadow for eventual replacement of the doomed giant.

When you return to the footpath, walk ahead to #7726 and turn left. On the left, across from #7724, is a horse-chestnut growing in such a tight rock crevice that it could only have been planted by a squirrel or bluejay. Happy accidents of this sort may contribute more to the atmosphere of natural woodland than any planting contrived by man, and also serve as proof that even in a city, the forces of nature operate to keep a forest in a state of constant renewal.

Look to the right to the rather odd bracket planting of shrubs that defines the corners of a rectangle of turf. This was the site of a croquet field, fenced off at the request of a private club. The fence was removed as a result of organized public protest and the meadow is now restored to the enjoyment of all park visitors.

Directly ahead where the path ends in a T is a *Sophora japonica* dividing into three trunks about 5 feet above ground. A flourishing family of saplings and seedlings behind the parent tree and across the path provides another example of a forest perpetuating itself.

The sophora's lacy canopy is composed of pinnately compound leaves with oval leaflets. A dependable all-season mark of identification is the olive green bark of recent shoots, the color persisting on growth as much as four years old. The sassafras also has green shoots but has simple, not compound, leaves. The pale tan bark of the sophora helps to distinguish it from other members of the pea family, the black and honey locusts and the yellow-wood. The sophora's flowering time, from July until September, and its long, lumpy, pale green seed pods, are unique features of this beautiful immigrant which accommodates itself so gracefully to life in a western city.

Take the path to the left. Twenty feet ahead on the right is a silverbell, *Halesia carolina*, with a large and a smaller trunk from the same base. This ornamental tree is a native of our southern highlands but is capable of establishing itself and starting a family in the North. The tree takes its name from the numerous bell-shaped flowers that hang in clusters along every shoot in May. The flowers are scentless and not so pure a white as those of the related *Styrax japonica*, but the halesia is more tree-like, and a little hardier. Its flowers are followed by large inflated capsules with four vertical wings on the sides.

123

Olmsted and Vaux created the Ramble to present an idealized native woodland. Understory plants like halesia make a graceful transition between underbrush and towering forest trees and should be used generously to contribute to an atmosphere of natural luxuriance.

Walk past the halesia to lamp post #7634. A little farther ahead on the left, a hackberry is attempting to swallow a boulder as an amoeba engulfs its prey. Walk on just past #7632 where another ambitious tree, this time a black cherry, has set itself to devour a rock.

A few steps ahead, take a right turn around a group of Japanese hollies, *Ilex crenata,* a gloomy black-green at best and made even more funereal by a coating of city soot. These alien, unconforming shrubs are as much out of place in a naturalistic planting as the halesia is at home.

Just beyond the hollies, on the right bank, is a thicket of sassafras with many youngsters springing up in a cycle of renewal. The bark of new sassafras shoots is a slightly paler green than that of the sophora seen earlier, and in addition has a powdery coating like the bloom on a grape. The diversely formed, sometimes mitten-shaped leaves are easily distinguished from the sophora's feathery compound leaves.

Just before you come to the next fork, in the curve of the path to the left, is a mulberry which outdoes the sassafras in variability of leaf patterns. Shiny leaves indicate that this is the oriental white mulberry, *Morus alba,* valued as food for silkworms and originally brought to this country in the hope of starting a domestic silk industry. The experiment failed but the white mulberry flourished and is, with the ailanthus, the commonest introduced weed tree in the metropolitan area. The native red mulberry, *Morus rubra,* whose leaves are rough as sandpaper on the upper surface, is a restrained spreader and is not encountered on any of our tours.

124

The Heart of the Ramble

Bear right around #7640. On both sides of the path are newly planted groups of red chokeberry, *Aronia arbutifolia*, a native shrub with a preference for full sun and moist situations. Its pink buds open to dainty white flowers like miniature apple blossoms but with a fringe of dark red stamens to add character. Leaves turn a brilliant scarlet late in the fall, and bright red berries prolong the warm color after the leaves have fallen.

If the aronias are not in flower or fruit, you can check the identification by examining the leaves with a hand lens. On the upper side of the leaf, the mid-vein is studded with tiny hairlike glands in a staggered row, alternately pointing left and right. In addition you will find persistent stipules (leaflike processes at the base of the leafstalk) which are characteristic of the rose family to which the aronia belongs.

Opposite lamp post #7642 is a bench, and about 8 feet behind its far end is an Asian shrub of exceptional interest, *Eleagnus multiflora*, so poorly sited that it is certain to be overlooked. Its leaves at first glance look somewhat like those of privet, but if you examine them closely, you will find the edges waved and the undersides lustrous and beautifully silvered. The oblong, translucent fruit is distinctively colored, a smoky amber ripening to carnelian, and is minutely speckled with what appear under a hand lens as clear bubbles of air. This shrub is the only one of its kind I've found in Central Park. Certainly others should be given a place in the sun where they can be readily admired.

Continue walking ahead past the little clearing on your right. At its far end, in the angle of the crosswalk at the right, is a picturesquely twisted catalpa with branches dipping over the path. Because of their huge leaves, the catalpa and paulownia are often confused. However, in midsummer when the catalpa bears its showy trusses of white flowers, it is easily distinguished

125

from the paulownia which has violet flowers in May. The catalpa's long thin beans are quite distinct from the paulownia's pecanlike capsules. If all these signs fail, look for leaf scars: the paulownia has opposite leaves in pairs, while the catalpa produces leaves in a whorl of three.

Continue straight ahead past the crosswalk and stop at the next large tree close to the path on the left. This is a swamp white oak, *Quercus bicolor*, with round-lobed, white-hairy leaves that broaden towards the tip. Acorns are borne in pairs on a long stalk but as they are sweet and much favored by squirrels, you may search a long time before you find one.

The brook usually overflows the path ahead, to the great delight of birds that bathe in the shallow water but at some inconvenience to lightly shod walkers. Instead of crossing the puddle, stop to study the planting in the vicinity of the oak. The rangy shrub whose branches touch the oak on the far side is a spicebush, *Lindera benzoin*, with aromatic twigs and leaves. Yellow flowers, small but profuse, cover the naked twigs in March. Foliage turns a uniform light yellow in autumn. The spicebush grows by choice in wet places, sometimes on tussocks in shallow ponds, a companion of skunk cabbage and cinnamon ferns. It is ideally suited to this brookside planting.

The low broad-leafed evergreens on the meadow border are less well sited. These are *Rhododendron carolinianum*, a delightful shrub with powderpuffs of white, pink, or rose flowers and a good compact habit. This native of our southern highlands likes cool, moist, well-aerated soil but abhors wet feet. It is not likely to succeed where its roots encounter standing water, as is possible in this low-lying spot.

The route now leaves the path and follows the course of the Gill to the south. In case the grass is too wet for

126

comfortable walking, you can skip the meadow and detour by path to the huge cork trees behind the benches, where you can pick up the tour.

About eight feet south of the swamp white oak, we come next to a sorrel tree, *Oxydendrum arboreum,* the choice wildling we first saw alongside the Boat House railing. In this congenial spot, it should develop into an outstanding ornament. To its left are two little sour gums, probably suckers from the roots of the larger specimen at the water's edge, behind the second youngster. The next large tree is a red maple, again happily sited and adding its polychrome autumn finery to the varied reds of oxydendrum and sour gum.

This planting follows almost word for word Olmsted's plan for making the Ramble a garden of American plants: "The present growth, consisting of sweet gum, spicebush, tulip-tree, sassafras, red-maple, black-oak, azalea, andromeda (pieris) etc., is exceedingly intricate and interesting." However, to produce "a much more natural wild character in the interior views," he directs that "much greater variety and more interest of detail is to be introduced" in the form of evergreens, ferns, mosses, and wild bulbs. As we circle the little pool, we shall see how these instructions have been observed in recent years.

Follow the course of the Gill until you come to a path. Behind the benches on its far side are two colossal cork trees, superlative specimens with marvelously corded bark and wide-spreading limbs. These are both males of the hairless type, *Phellodendron amurense* var. *amurense,* rarely found in Central Park. As you face these trees, turn left and walk about 80 feet to see a female of the same variety, a smaller tree loaded in season with juicy black fruit and eager birds. Opposite the female cork tree, a few feet off the path, is another sorrel tree, this one about 15 feet high, old enough to show its distinctive drooping flower or fruit sprays.

127

After this short detour, return to stand before the two giant cork trees. When this tour was first scouted, it was apparent that both trees were in critical need of attention. Both had many dead limbs and incorrectly cut stubs. The smaller one on the right was in especially bad condition from crowding and shading. The larger tree has a low branch stretching to the east. One fork of the branch was torn off in the February 1969 snowstorm, leaving a foot-long split below the crotch. A generous gift to the Camperdown Fund from Mrs. Henry L. Moses provided skilled care for the cork trees and for the styrax we shall see presently.

The Bartlett men, on examining the break, declared that the branch was too badly damaged to save and advised cutting it off. I felt the loss of the branch would alter the whole character of the tree and—for the first and only time—I overrode professional opinion by insisting that it at least be given a chance. My decision was strengthened by evidence that cork trees are highly resistant to rot. Even when long-dead limbs were taken off, the cut showed clean, sound wood (surprisingly, bright canary yellow) without a trace of decay. On the debit side, it appears that healing is slow, judging by the very small collar of new bark that had formed around the base of stubs.

I assured the Bartlett foreman, Henry Kreuzer, that I would take full responsibility for sparing the injured limb and that if the gamble failed, it would not reflect on his judgment. The trees have been thoroughly pruned and the weakened limb supported by a cable. The split should be reinforced with a bolt but this, and root feeding, must wait until spring.

Work on the cork trees was carried out in ankle-deep snow on December 29. Because paths had not been ploughed, the truck had to be left at the Boat House and all the gear—ladder, saws, ropes, cables, and tools—

carried on foot up the slippery hill. At the time, telephone service in the city had broken down. When inability to communicate was added to unfavorable weather, we all agreed most heartily to call it quits for the season.

The lower limbs of the tree on the right were all dead and had to be removed, leaving a rather ordinary, upright branching structure. By contrast, you can realize how vital the low branch is to the dramatic horizontality of the larger tree. As I have said, the decision to spare the limb rests on my shoulders. Perhaps it can be saved; perhaps its loss is merely postponed. Meanwhile, I hope that all walkers in the Ramble will serve as deputy tree wardens to keep an eye on the patient and notify me if there is any change in its condition.

Across from the cork trees, at the water's edge, is an unnatural straight line of azaleas, the garish carmine 'Hinode-giri,' an offense to the eye in almost any garden setting and a shrieking dissonance in this quiet spot. Olmsted clearly described his plan for the Ramble: "There can be no better place than the Ramble for the perfect realization of the wild garden and I want to stock it in that way as fully and as rapidly as is possible." Instead of gaudy exotics, any of our native azaleas would be better suited: the early flowering, delicate mauve *Rhododendron vaseyi*, the spicily scented *RR. roseum* and *nudiflorum*, or the white *R. viscosum* to fill the summer air with fragrance.

Farther ahead on the right are two red maples. Continue past them and turn left at lamp post #7541. Behind the bench ahead on the left is a grove of *Cornus kousa*, an Asian dogwood. This is a valuable small tree, blooming in late May and early June, a full month after our native flowering dogwood, *C. florida*, and far more tolerant of city conditions. Unlike our native woodlander, the Chinese dogwood wants full sun. These shaded trees, spindly and sparse flowering, give little idea of their

129

potential beauty. If you have seen the Chinese dogwood properly grown, with a dense head and great drooping fans of branches, you would want to see it widely planted in the park, especially to replace monotonous and garden-like flowering crabs and cherries.

The petallike bracts of the Chinese dogwood are pointed, not notched at the end like those of our native. They are a cool greenish white, very refreshing against the deep green of the leaves. The fruit also is distinctive. Unlike *Cornus florida's* clusters of shiny scarlet berries, *C. kousa* has dangling rose-red balls like velvet-covered cherries. As a final novelty, note the flaking, many-colored bark, more like a London plane's than a conventional dogwood's.

The path turns left at a rock cliff. About 20 feet beyond the turn, on the left side, is a small tree showing orange patches under flaking bark and with three suckers at its base. This is *Styrax japonica*, a faultless tree, refined and lovely in every detail. Trimly designed, clean, unwilting foliage gives an air of elegance throughout the growing season. The styrax reaches a peak of delight on Memorial Day when its branches are hung with pure white bells with protruding yellow stamens for clappers and breathing a seductive fragrance. As you walk under the arching branches to admire the flowers against the sky, I'm sure you will agree that the styrax is worthy of the highest praise.

The specimen is past its prime. Its trunk is hollow. Obviously it is not worth expensive repairs. Still, remembering the singular joy of coming on the tree by accident and standing entranced under its bower of bloom, I asked the Bartlett men to clean up the worst of the split and jagged branches. After all, who wants to be sensible all the time?

As I was skidding around on the crusted snow, helping to pick up pruned wood in an effort to get warm, I found

130

another styrax in the woods behind and to the left of this specimen. The trunk appears to be entirely dead but there are a number of suckers at the base. If the trunk were cut away and one or two of the strongest suckers retained, the tree might reconstitute itself. This work couldn't be done in 1969 as it wasn't included in the permit but we'll certainly take a closer look in spring and add it to the list if the roots appear to be sound.

Moderate-growing trees of this sort—*Styrax japonica, Cornus kousa,* fringe tree, and the coral-fruited spiny ash, *Zanthoxylum simulans,* not found in Central Park—should be used to replace the many European hornbeams dead or dying as a result of drought. This styrax should be kept alive as a sample until others are established. Once seen by those who would like to contribute plants to Central Park, the styrax might help to prevent the simplicity of Olmsted's pastoral landscape from being drowned in a gaudy purple-pink flood of 'Kwanzan' cherries.

Beyond the styrax, guideposts give out entirely. Since it is impossible to direct a further advance, let's backtrack to the little stone bridge over the Gill and cross it. Immediately on the right of the path we come on a patch of evergreen barberries, *Berberis julianae.* This Chinese shrub is an outstanding subject for formal plantings but totally alien to the atmosphere of an American woodland and, quite obviously, unable to compete with a lusty growth of weeds. Money that is annually thrown away on predictable failures might better be used to engage a landscape architect with knowledge of ecology as well as extensive training in historical landscaping.

Set among the barberries are three corkscrew willows, *Salix matsudana tortuosa.* These are out-and-out freaks, disrupting the woodland atmosphere with their frantically contorted outlines, and marking a new low in the level of planting in Central Park.

In 1869 Clarence Cook, with his usual faultless taste,

observed approvingly that "an effort has been made to bring into these bounds as many of the wood flowers and flowering shrubs, the native growths of our forests, as would thrive here—foreign flowers and imported shrubs being put in places more seemingly artificial."

In accordance with the idea of collecting native shrubs, this would be an ideal spot to introduce *Cyrilla racemiflora* to an appreciative public. This shrub is virtually unknown but of exceptional decorative merit. Its long, shining, leathery leaves are evergreen in the South. In our area they turn brilliant deep red in late autumn and remain in splendor until after the end of the year. White flowers in fingerlike spikes are followed by drooping tan seed pods, quite persistent, and somewhat suggestive of the fruit of *Oxydendrum arboreum*.

Just beyond the barberries is a good thicket of *Aronia arbutifolia*, the red chokeberry we saw earlier, here thriving in a congenially moist spot.

The chokeberry thicket gives way to a mess of Japanese barberry, *Berberis thunbergii*, the utterly banal, common, snag-your-stocking hedge plant of city and suburban yards. The use of barberry in the Ramble is a needless affront. Clarence Cook wrote in 1869, "The design in planting the Ramble has been to give, if possible, the delicate flavor of wildness so hard to seize and imprison when civilization has once put it to flight." Our woods and watersides are rich in shrubs with the flavor of wildness—clethra, blueberry, buttonbush, azaleas, shadbush, fothergilla to name a few. The choice of barberry betrays every standard of taste, fitness, and imagination.

There's more to come: a stretch of misshapen, sickly hawthorns, upland trees that make weak growth on wet soil. Despite the evident failure of hawthorns in this environment, others have recently been planted as replacements. It would have been wiser to use a plant that grows by choice on the banks of bogs and ditches: the sweet bay, *Magnolia virginiana*. Its beautiful white-backed leaves, intensely fragrant white flowers in June, and handsome red fruit make it a delightful ornament for the waterside.

Clarence Cook spoke with high praise of *M. virginiana*, in his day extensively used in the Ramble. It is one of the rare native plants which, he predicted, would grow in value to teachers of botany as accessible wild areas on the outskirts of the city became increasingly built up.

Walk ahead but instead of crossing the stream, keep left and start up the hill beside the miniature rapids. This is a key spot, the source of the Gill, one that calls for sensitive planting and scrupulous maintenance. To create the illusion of a natural spring, water should gush from a mysterious cavern draped with shrubs and creepers. The piled-up rocks above and beside it need a luxuriant mantle of greenery to disguise their artificial construction.

Those who know and love the woods will recognize the wonderful opportunity for sympathetic handling of the Ramble, especially the pivotal area of the Gill. Artists, birders, and botanists who are drawn to this wildlife sanctuary should join forces to obtain informed care for this city-dweller's Eden.

Continue up the hill, cross a footpath, and walk into the loveliest glade in Central Park, a tree-enclosed meadow brought to life by a superbly placed sour gum set among rocks. This is the goal of the tour, an invitation to linger in sun or shade, to breathe the air of repose, and to admire the clarity and simplicity of design that mark Olmsted's genius. There are flaws: the senseless addition of a small tree on the left which interferes with the view of the sour gum and which should be moved elsewhere, and the London planes planted like street trees along the path to the north. Despite these alterations, the serenity of the glade is unspoiled. The sour gum on its artless throne might be its presiding spirit. If you think

I am indulging in fancy, consider that Humphrey Marshall, the eighteenth century plantsman who described the tree, named it *Nyssa sylvatica*, or woodland water nymph. When contemplating a beautiful sour gum, even a sober botanist can be moved to poetry.

The Ramble is a freeform maze. Getting lost in it is half the fun. As the paths look much alike, you may find yourself getting lost a different way every time. If you head downhill, you'll eventually come out on the Lake —near the Boat House if you bear east, over some bridges and out to Central Park West and 77th Street if you bear west.

If you are still keen for adventure, take the path to the north under the London planes, then up some steps to the left, and approach a fairytale castle, the Belvedere, by a secret pass over a bridge hewn from solid rock. From the Belvedere terrace you can sight a landmark and make your way back to the city like a returning explorer, trailing a delicate aura of wildness.

> "Our park is not for the present day alone, but for all the generations yet to come; and if the generous people of New York shall be remembered and blessed by their posterity for any good deed, above all others it will be for this inestimable gift."
>
> *T. Addison Richards*
> *in Harper's New Monthly Magazine, August 1861.*

134

IX

OSAGE OASIS

Sixth Avenue and Central Park South

Oₙ this tour we shall see the most magnificent Osage orange in Central Park and add a yellowwood, American holly, and *Aralia elata* to our list. The yellowwood is one of the valued summer-flowering peas. To enjoy its fragrant flowers, time the walk for the last days of May. If you want a reason for a second visit, come in September when the aralia is topped by enormous plumes of white flowers.

The southern part of Central Park has been largely obliterated by encroachments. Acres of parkland and water have been buried under buildings or turned into asphalt deserts. Because former open spaces are withdrawn from general use, pressure on the remaining natural areas is aggravated. Hillsides are trampled to bare clay and tree roots are damaged by erosion and compaction. The landscape has been so gravely defaced that it was possible to chart only one tour starting from Central Park South.

This is a tour for active champions of the park, for conservationists impelled by "a sense of honest outrage," in the phrase of John B. Oakes of *The New York Times*. Without a doubt, the route covers the worst planted and worst maintained area I have found. The tour is justified only by its goal, a miraculously unspoiled bowl-shaped meadow backed by a cliff for windbreak and dominated by a superlative Osage orange.

As you face the park, take the path on the right side of Center Drive and follow its curve along the margin of the road, stopping 5 feet short of lamp post #C5907. In June, a trailing rose with single pink flowers—probably the variety 'Max Graf'—was charmingly draped over the rocky margin of the walk. Though a hybrid, the rose has the simplicity of a wildflower. It was later slashed back to a few stubs.

On the hillside above the mutilated rose is a good low-branching specimen of *Euonymus alatus*, called winged euonymus for the curious corky flanges that line its twigs, and Burning Bush for its glorious rose-red autumn foliage and scarlet fruits. The impact of rich color is most effective when this Asian euonymus is grown in closely massed thickets. Since it is easily available, it should be used generously to clothe bare slopes such as this one.

Walk ahead to the near end of the first bench. Behind it, 20 feet up the rise, is a species rose from Japan, *Rosa multiflora*, a tough, adaptable wildling extensively used in barrier planting, erosion control, and for wildlife

136

refuges. Its thickly interlaced tangles of semi-erect, thorny canes make safe nesting sites for birds and sanctuaries for small game. Persistent red hips are relished by birds and animals alike. Small white flowers in pyramidal clusters add a modest decorative note in midsummer. This specimen is admirably related to a boulder which supports the canes and is softened by their tracery.

In contrast to this wholly satisfying, natural-looking group is the sprawly, two-trunked tree just to its left on the hillside. This is *Albizzia julibrissin* var. *rosea*, called silk tree or, more commonly, mimosa—the latter a double-barreled misnomer referring to the fluffy yellow flowers sold by florists as mimosa but which are in fact acacia. A native of Persia, albizzia is now found chiefly in the back yards of suburban housing developments. It is totally alien to a naturalistic landscape, especially when its flimsiness is accentuated by association with massive rock cliffs.

The albizzia has enormous, drooping, fernlike leaves, doubly compound, with tiny leaflets. Because of weak, pithy wood and the weight and wind resistance of its foliage, albizzias are easily broken by storms and seldom achieve much height. The albizzia belongs to the pea family but you would never guess the relationship from its flowers which look like rose-pink shaving brushes and smell like ripe watermelon. Flowers appear in July, continue over a long season, and are followed by tan pods. The albizzia is very late in leafing out and should not be planted where its rangy bare branches will detract from the effect of a spring garden.

Walk ahead to lamp post #C5909. The rocks on the right were blasted during road building. In comparison with the weathered contours of glacier-smoothed outcrops, these fractured edges are unpleasantly jagged. They were not intended to be left bare. Olmsted gave specific orders that "rock edges and clefts at various points, particularly . . . on both sides of the drive near the Sixth Avenue entrance . . . are to be dressed with peat and wood earth and planted with ferns, mosses, and Alpine plants." I shouldn't like to entrust such fragile plants to today's untutored visitors. However, the asphalt could be removed to make crannies at the base for sticky-fingered vines such as Virginia creeper, while twiners like trumpet vine, akebia, *Clematis paniculata*, or porcelain vine could be planted at the top and coaxed to festoon the rocks below.

Beyond the rocks is a planting of *Rosa rugosa*, an Asian species that takes its name from the rough, crinkled texture of the leaves. The deep rose or crimson flowers have the rich, heady fragrance of old-fashioned roses and are an important ingredient in potpourri as well as a source of honey. These rather leggy shrubs are not so well suited to dressing a rough slope as limber *R. multiflora*, so snugly draped over a rocky cushion.

In this case, the canes of the rugosas have been unnaturally stretched by competition with ailanthus saplings and polygonum. With alert maintenance, the ailanthus seedlings would have been tweaked out when they first appeared, a matter of twenty minutes' work. Instead, the saplings were allowed to get a firm root hold and grew until they overtopped the roses. These saplings were cut down in the fall of 1969, leaving stumps 2 and 3 inches in diameter. Ailanthus isn't to be disposed of so easily: new shoots will sprout vigorously from trunks and roots. This growth will have to be killed with an herbicide applied with a sponge or paintbrush, a ticklish and time-consuming job, but necessary where spray might drift and kill the roses. The same technique, even more delicately controlled, must be used on the polygonum which has thrust its shoots right through the base of some of the rosebushes.

Walk ahead to the traffic light and lamp post #C5911.

138

Fifteen feet to the right is a thicket of *Aralia elata*, the Japanese angelica tree. The name perhaps derives from a remote resemblance to the herb angelica, a member of the carrot family. Certainly it's hard to imagine anything less angelic than this ferociously armed tree with spines not only on trunk and young shoots but on the leafstalks and between each pair of leaflets. Its American cousin, *A. spinosa*, has the more fitting common names of Hercules' Club and Devil's Walking Stick.

Like the Kentucky coffee tree and albizzia, the aralia has doubly compound leaves. The complete leaf, with its side stalks and long narrow leaflets, can reach a length of 4 feet or more. Unlike the spindly albizzia, the aralia makes a solidly based clump strengthened by a flourishing crop of suckers. It is in fact an invasive tree, not for select spots where its rampant increase would menace more delicate plants, but ideal for a rough spot among rocks. In August and September it flaunts enormous terminal plumes of off-white flowers. These are followed by small black fruits, quickly stripped by birds. The stalks that supported the inflorescence then turn a soft mulberry-rose and look at a distance like a cloud of tiny flowers.

Because of the aralia's arsenal of prickles, it makes an impassable barrier, more effective than chain link fencing and far more decorative. In flower and leaf, the aralia has the tropical look that Olmsted prized and strove to achieve, especially in lakeside plantings. Do you recall looking north from the Hernshead? (page 62) The view was marred by a hillock streaked with trampled paths of yellow clay. A number of *Aralia elata* planted at the water's edge would discourage landing parties and restore the unbroken luxuriance of foliage that was intended to frame the Lake.

Between the aralia and another lanky albizzia, standing on its thin leg like a balancing stork, lie 50 feet of desolation. The stark rock cliff and the shelf below it cry out for large-scale planting. *Hydrangea anomela* var. *petiolaris,* capable of scaling a 60 foot wall, would soon dress this rather featureless rock face with its bold, shining, dark green leaves and brackets of flat, white flower clusters in July. The climbing hydrangea is not evergreen but its thick red-brown stems and ivory buds hold great interest in winter. It is an immensely vigorous woody vine with just the look of force and vitality needed to match the bulk of the cliff.

For planting on the ledge below the cliff, I think of the ground-sweeping *Crataegus nitida,* the well-named shining hawthorn, whose glossy, deep green leaves set off clusters of large white flowers. The evergreen, orange-fruited pyracantha, so strangely absent from Central Park, is another. However, it's useless to name a few plants when the whole area needs redesigning according to a comprehensive, unified plan by a landscape architect well grounded in ecology, plant materials, and Olmsted's directions for creating a naturalistic landscape.

As you walk ahead, you will come to a rocky shelf on the right where a red or swamp maple, *Acer rubrum,* finds a narrow foothold. Doubtless sprung from windblown seed and stunted by hardship, it nevertheless clings to life in this uncongenial spot, with each twist in its trunk expressing the drama of struggle.

Farther along on the right is a well-established American holly, *Ilex opaca.* The dull-surfaced leaves of the American holly are much less attractive than the shining foliage of English holly but the American is both hardier and more treelike. In favorable situations, especially in the South, it may grow as tall as 100 feet. It is unique in being the only broad-leafed evergreen tree that is reliably hardy in the North. A very few individuals of the southern magnolia, *M. grandiflora,* grow in Brooklyn—witness the notable specimen on Lafayette Avenue—but the foliage of most is browned or killed over winter so the tree can't truly be classed as evergreen in our climate.

This American holly is a male which of course bears no fruit and has escaped being torn to pieces for Christmas decoration. The holly is flanked by several large mock oranges, an excellent grouping with good contrast and feeling for scale.

Beyond the semicircular rock, grooved like a phonograph record, is an extraordinary mishmash of baby shrubs apparently planted on the blunderbuss principle: if enough kinds are planted, one of them may turn out to be right. Among the waifs are—or were—*Cotoneaster horizontalis, Berberis triacanthophora,* and the half-hardy holly, *Ilex cornuta 'Burfordii'*—all worthy plants in the right place but here mostly dead of shade, erosion, or trampling. If this planting was intended to block a short cut down the rocks, it would have been more effective to put in two or three large specimens of cockspur thorn or the steel-spined hardy orange, *Poncirus trifoliata.* To add to the disorder, daffodils have been stuck among the assorted shrubs. The bold vertical leaves and flower stalks of the bulbs make a jarring disruption in the already spotty planting.

Trumpet daffodils—obvious garden hybrids—are not adapted to naturalizing even when planted in meadows where grass can grow tall and mask the ripening bulb foliage. Wild bulbs are more harmonious in a wild setting. *Scilla sibirica* or *Chionodoxa gigantea,* planted in well-filled rock crevices, would make a blue waterfall over outcrops and seed themselves into pools on the ledges. These are small scale, rock hugging alpines, flowering just after the last snow and taking themselves away neatly soon afterwards.

Starting with a dying two-trunked European hornbeam 15 feet up the rise, the trees along this walk and in the section to the east are in such wretched condition that I hesitate to list them. I had found a honey locust barbed along its trunk with branched spines, and a cork tree and ailanthus growing close together so that their differences could be established. These and many other trees in the area are in critical condition, as evidenced by dead crowns and branches and by severe bark lesions. The environment has deteriorated to the point of being unable to support tree life.

If radical steps are not taken, this area will soon be a desert. A qualified consultant should be called in to study the total ecology: to make soil tests, chart trees to be removed as hopelessly damaged, direct treatment for the survivors, select trees for replacement, and—perhaps most important—advise on fences or protective shrub plantings. There is no possibility of growing anything on these slopes as long as hordes of visitors are permitted to ignore footpaths and to pound the soil to concrete.

It is regrettable that owners of the great hotels on Central Park South are not alarmed by the imminent death of southern Central Park—perhaps not even aware of it. In contrast, residents on Fifth Avenue are keenly and actively involved in the preservation of the park. They are becoming increasingly vocal in demanding intelligent maintenance of the city's most vital open green space.

A suggested solution is to place the two acknowledged masterpieces of landscaping art, Central and Prospect Park, under a separate administration, perhaps patterned after the Brooklyn Institute of Arts and Sciences which embraces the Brooklyn Museum, Academy of Music, Botanic Garden, and Children's Museum. Each of these institutions has its own director, a man chosen from among the most distinguished specialists in his field, not for political or social connections. Each of our historic parks deserves a director of the same professional eminence: a man with wide experience in administration, horticulture, public education, and the training of personnel. Unless a

142

large number of determined citizens exert their influence to improve the quality of park management, the landscape may be devastated beyond recall.

Walk ahead to the next intersection where a path branches off to the right. Look down the path to one of the grossest encroachments in Central Park, a skating rink that reduced the northern arm of the Pond to a fetid, cement-walled ditch. Gentle-spoken Calvert Vaux had a harsh word for such barbarities: "Every attempt to force individual buildings into prominent notice is an evidence either of a vulgar desire for notoriety at any sacrifice, or of an ill-educated eye and taste."

The hulking structure is condemned primarily for destroying an essential sheet of water, but its malign influence extends far beyond its physical boundaries. In summer, for commercially sponsored concerts with paid admission, the rink is topped by a tower of glaring metal pipes and canvas screens. The pastoral atmosphere of the whole southeastern end of the park is disrupted by this visual pollution, while amplified racket makes the nights hideous for those who live nearby.

From the very inception of Central Park, when water was let into the unfinished Lake in 1858, ice skating was its most popular activity, drawing greater crowds than came for relief on summer's hottest day. According to Olmsted's figures, 500,000 skaters crowded Central Park's frozen lakes and ponds in a single week, with as many as 100,000 on a single day. It was to accommodate the tremendous demands for skating space that Olmsted and Vaux made Prospect Park's lake more than twice as large as Central Park's.

In the skating season, temporary shelters were placed around the Lake, with sheds for renting skates and checking shoes, while lights were set on tall poles to illuminate the ice at night. As old prints show, it was a marvelously animated and festive scene. It could have been continued,

143

even in our warmer winters, by the use of technical ingenuity such as the New York Philharmonic employs in bringing fine music to the park without defacing the landscape. The Pond, like Conservatory Water, could have been piped for artificial freezing with, at worst, a small building to house machinery. In this way, skaters could have enjoyed their sport in the freedom of a natural setting, without obtruding on the beauty of the park which is the basic pleasure and right of all visitors in every season. The donor of a nearly invisible facility which preserved the Pond as an integral part of the landscape would have been held in highest honor as long as the park endures.

Now that we've seen a shattering example of how a park is destroyed, let's walk on to see what makes it eminently worth saving. Continue ahead past the traffic light and cross Driprock Arch. Fifty feet ahead on the right, a superb Osage orange stands on a knoll. Usually an irregularly shaped tree, this giant has majestic balance, solidly based on a monumental spread of buttress roots, and with a gracefully dipping branch that follows the contour of the slope. This tree, shown in Peet as part of the original planting, has a circumference of 9′2″ measured taut at 4 feet above grade and is by far the largest and handsomest specimen in Central Park. It is a male tree so you needn't hesitate to walk under its branches to study their pattern against the sky, and to admire the channeled orange trunk and sculptural roots.

The little meadow owes its charm to this tree, the only one of consequence in the picture. While the tree appears to be in flourishing condition, its age and importance in the landscape warrant every encouragement to keep it in health.

I've referred to the work of the Friends of Central Park

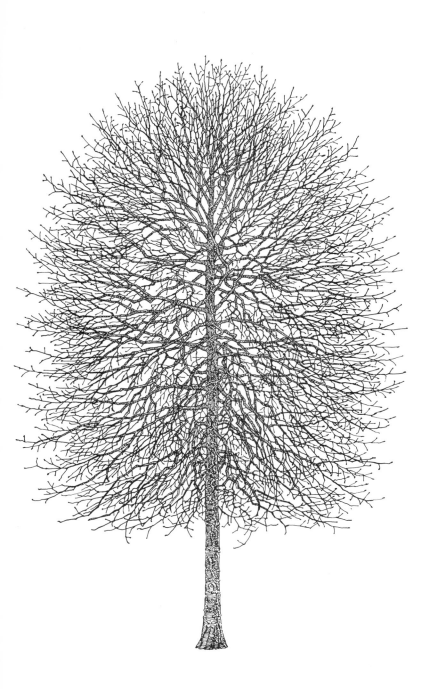

in restoring trees, but without really explaining what the program is or how it began. In 1967 the Friends of Prospect Park started a program of tree restoration called the Camperdown Fund after its most illustrious patient, the Camperdown elm. The Bartlett Tree Company was engaged to prune, fill, cable, and feed a number of the park's historic trees threatened by long neglect. Money was raised through voluntary contributions and by the sale of note paper with park-related designs. The program, now in its fourth year, will be continued until Prospect Park has a qualified horticultural director to take over the job.

In the miles of scouting that went into preparation of this book, the sorry condition of Central Park's trees became painfully obvious. A companion program was proposed by the Friends of Central Park and, in a mood of optimism in no way reflecting the funds on hand, eleven trees were selected as candidates for restoration. (One of these was later canceled as beyond repair.) The opportunity to participate in the salvage of trees met with such eager public response that all ten trees were treated in 1969 and there is a small nest egg to apply to work in 1970.

Since mounting pollution creates a hostile environment, it is unlikely that today's young trees will ever attain the size of those that made their growth before automobiles, oil burners, and incinerators fouled the air. For this reason, it is vital to preserve the surviving giants. Obviously the most seriously threatened trees must be given priority. Nevertheless, if the Central Park Camperdown Fund grows in popularity, I should like to supplement emergency rescue work with prevention, that is, to prune and feed outstanding specimens to keep them in flourishing health. This superlative Osage orange is by no means on

146

the urgent list, yet I believe it merits preventive care because of its dominant role in the landscape.*

Let's walk into the meadow now to savor its atmosphere of seclusion, incredibly preserved from the changes that have ravaged the surrounding landscape. The roadway is sufficiently elevated so that the noise and fumes of traffic are somewhat remote, and if you choose your viewpoint, you can avoid sight of the monstrous skating rink. At some future time when the park is cared for, it would be desirable to plant a thick tree screen across the southeast end of the meadow but it would be folly at present to put in new trees where existing ones are being killed by trampling.

The assortment of conifers at the top of the meadow has the impromptu look that might result from driving a truckload of trees around the park and dropping them off in empty places like a cuckoo laying its eggs. The combination of larches with pines is an unfortunate one. It is quite natural for larches to lose their needles in winter but when they stand bare among evergreen trees, they appear dead, not merely dormant, and the unity of the group is broken.

The unfamiliar tree with broad, flattened needles grooved on both sides is *Sciatopitys verticillata,* the Japanese umbrella pine, so called because its needles are arranged in whorls like the ribs of an umbrella. This is an exceedingly handsome tree with dense, lustrous foliage and a formal, columnar habit of growth. Its use in the city is still experimental but if it proves able to survive, it will be a valuable addition to the short list of tolerant evergreen trees. The third conifer is *Pinus koraiensis,* the

* A welcome contribution from the Francis E. Fowler, Jr., Foundation of Los Angeles, has assured the rejuvenation of the Osage orange. The gift was made in recognition of Central Park's status as a supreme example of American art.

Korean pine, grown successfully on Long Island but still to be tested for ability to survive city conditions.

On the northeast side, the right-angled opposition of lawn and cliff is unpleasantly abrupt. The bald dome of rock looms over the meadow like a stranded whale. Since it lacks the deep striations and crevices that give sculptural quality to many Central Park rocks, it would be improved by a tracery of vines to make a shadow pattern on its flat surface. This would be the perfect spot for Virginia creeper, *Parthenocissus quinquefolia,* a vigorous native with blue berries much favored by birds, and with flamboyant autumn color to dress the rock with a sheet of fire. An irregular mass of the red-fruited, red-foliaged *Photinia villosa* we admired on East Meadow would carry out the brilliant autumn color scheme and mask the harsh line of the rock's base. This is the kind of landscape-integrated planting that should be suggested to donors instead of the superimposed, extraneous prettiness of Japanese cherries and beds of flowering garden shrubs.

Donors who confuse flowers with landscaping might be indulged in this meadow. If the grass is left uncut until midsummer, a naturalized planting of wild bulbs would be charming—not of course in dense clots according to the Victorian taste for bedding-out, but in loose drifts advancing from under the black cherries and among the pines, thinning out and then gathering into random groups as if the wind had scattered their seed. The slender, dancing, heaven-scented poet's narcissus with its white wings and short red-rimmed cup is enchanting in grass; so is the summer snowflake, *Leucojum aestivum,* which looks like a mammoth lily-of-the-valley on a 2 foot stem. Both of these prefer moist situations but should endure if long grass shades their roots. For a sure thing, plant the jaunty, irrepressible little weed, *Ornithogalum umbellatum,* the Star of Bethlehem that covers the hillsides of Prospect Park with a late snow. Children gather it by the grubby fistful but its increase below ground more than makes up for loss of seed. This is not a plant for well-ordered gardens but its green-backed white stars are entirely appropriate in wild places such as this artless meadow and the glades in the Ramble.

One of the most inviting aspects of this south-facing hollow is its ability to trap the sun's warmth while blocking the north wind. Even in mid-winter you'll find people sunning themselves in the lee of the cliff, and many find the first promise of spring in the strengthening sun rays that pierce the cold air. If you spend a quiet hour here, refreshed and in tune with nature, you'll absorb the tranquil freedom that Central Park was designed to provide and which must be preserved at all cost.

When you're ready to return to the city, make your way back to the traffic light and cross the road. The immense tree with many burls on its trunk, 5 feet this side of the bridge parapet, is an English elm, *Ulmus procera.* Don't rely on the suckers on the trunk, as these are rarely typical, but look for a fallen leaf if you can't reach a branch. You have only to draw a finger over its upper surface to feel the short stubble that characterizes leaves of this tree, though you'll need a hand lens to see the soft hairs on the underside.

Two huge unpainted wounds on the south side of the trunk show an advanced state of decay. Failure to perform the simple but vital precaution of protecting all exposed wood with an annual coat of tree dressing will result in a weakening cavity and eventual loss of this splendid old tree. The Park Department now spends many man hours to plant and maintain flowers on Fifth and Park Avenues for the benefit of merchants and residents. Would not the time be more fittingly devoted to the care of parks which serve people from all parts of the city?

Opposite lamp post #C6202, in the angle of the intersecting paths, is a tree with smooth, pale gray bark that might be mistaken for that of beech. This is a yellow-wood, *Cladastris lutea*, another of our native peas and perhaps the most beautiful. It was discovered in Tennessee in 1796 by the French plantsman-explorer André Michaux and was later found in a very few scattered locations in the Middle South. Like the similarly restricted Osage orange, yellowwood has spread by cultivation and escape far beyond its original range. Again like Osage orange, yellowwood yields a yellow dye extracted from the inner bark of the roots by boiling. The wood, light, strong, and taking a high polish, was prized for making gunstocks. Now the tree is grown—and not so widely as it deserves—for its long clusters of flowers in the first days of June, flowers that look like rather loosely strung chains of white wisteria and carry the same entrancing fragrance.

Yellowwood has a unique feature that distinguishes it from other trees with pinnately compound leaves: its leaflets are arranged alternately on the central stalk. If you think of the others we've seen in the park—hickory, ash, locust, sophora, ailanthus, and the rest—you'll recall that their leaflets are set in pairs along the stalk. The yellowwood alone has leaflets in a staggered row, an unerring means of identification. Yellowwoods like rich woodsy soil. This specimen is handicapped by its position on a dry, packed ridge and may not flower freely. Look for a favorably situated specimen—there are numbers of them along East Drive—before you judge the decorative value of Michaux's treasured find.

As you head south, you pass a red oak and a pin oak. Beyond them on the hillside is a grove of black locust, *Robinia pseudo-acacia*, another native pea, seen at the Pool and again in the Ramble. You should recognize it easily by its deeply corded, tan-colored bark and—in May —by its tightly massed clusters of white flowers. The black locust has thorns in pairs at the base of leafstalks, a minor armament in comparison to the fierce spines of the honey locust which we shall see presently. Before we compare them, let me warn that the common names are totally misleading. The honey locust has near-black bark and inconspicuous scentless flowers; the black locust has tan bark and large fragrant flowers. The names should be reversed, and I do so, and then wrench them back, every time I must identify the trees. If you remember that the names are wrong, you'll be right.

As you walk forward past lamp post #C6002, look up to the top of the rise. Here are a number of honey locusts, *Gleditsia triacanthos,* with deep brown or black bark that breaks into large flat flakes on mature trunks. The formidable spines that bristle on trunk and branches bear secondary points, often in threes, as indicated by the name *triacanthos,* three-spined. A nearly spineless variety, less hazardous to passersby, is called *G. t. inermis,* which might be rendered as the disarmed three-spined gleditsia.

The leaflets of the honey locust are smaller than those of the black, and of heavier texture. Leaves are occasionally doubly compound. Flowers are greenish yellow, not pealike, and without decorative value, but they make up for small size by developing enormously long pods, 18 inches or more, red-brown, shining, and easily the most distinctive feature of the tree.

The stretch from here to Central Park South is extremely dull: Norway maples, ginkgos, and entirely too many straggly ailanthus. If all the female ailanthus in the area were eliminated, the problem of coping with unwanted seedlings would be solved, and there would be room to improve the quality of the planting.

If you're not in a hurry, walk up the grassy slope to the right of lamp post #C6002. Beyond the rocks on the far side of the rise, you'll find a contorted paulownia, a mere shell from untended wounds, but low-branched enough so that you can examine the curious tan buds,

151

prominent from late summer until they open to violet flowers in May.

To the right lies another blight on the pastoral landscape, less offensive than the skating rink only because of its lesser height. High fencing surrounds a flat, sun-baked waste of asphalt as inviting as the exercise yard of a prison. It is usually empty, while troops of jubilant children scale the rocky knoll to the north, one of the natural adventure playgrounds in which Central Park is rich.

The east side of the asphalt desert is oddly coupled to a pinched geometrical enclosure with a squat fountain in its center. When you recall Olmsted's goal, to obtain "the broadest effects of light and shade which can be obtained upon the ground, and to produce the impression of great space and freedom," you can only wonder at the mind that conceived this dank, oppressive cell and then, oblivious to the defacement of a work of art, proudly put his name on the gatepost.

Someday, we can dream, an enlightened philanthropist will earn everlasting fame by taking things *out* of Central Park. No plaque could be put on the work of tearing down fences, rolling up asphalt, and smashing concrete, but the benefactor's name would be lovingly remembered for the trees and open meadows and expanses of water he restored to Central Park.

> "Sometime, for the unexpected always happens, when the friends of the Park have become few and weak, or are sleeping at their posts, some great sweeping injury may come to Central Park through misguided undertakings and as an artistic unit New York will know it no more."
>
> *Samuel Parsons, Jr.*

X

THE WINTER DRIVE

90th Street and Central Park West

Tʜɪs tour is in the nature of a graduation party. On the assumption that you have gained a basic acquaintance with trees, it contains some fairly advanced material as well as frivolous but irresistible items that got crowded out of earlier walks.

The tour starts at 90th Street and Central Park West, follows the route of the Winter Drive, and ends at 88th Street. It is advisable to read the text before you start out. If, for instance, you are interested in learning how to prepare ginkgo nuts, you can do so more comfortably at home than standing in the park. If you are *not* interested in trying ginkgo nuts, you can find out ahead of time where to skip.

One thing you shouldn't skip, if you are to be an effective tree warden, is the discussion of how a tree lives—and, if it isn't given adequate care, how it dies. This is fairly meaty stuff but if you have it sorted out in your mind before you enter the park, you'll be able to recognize how good pruning speeds healing and bad pruning promotes decay.

The tour starts at a rather obscure gap in the wall about 100 feet north of 90th Street, directly opposite 300 Central Park West. When you enter the park, walk ahead towards the road and stop just before you cross. On the ridge at the right are three twisty-trunked shrubby trees, *Euonymus europeus,* a species that should be planted only if it will be conscientiously sprayed. These wretched specimens are so infested with aphids and scale insects that their leaves are deformed and their growth stunted. When properly grown, *E. europeus* is a glorious sight in autumn. Its foliage pales to ivory and then becomes flushed in various degrees with clear rose-pink. When the leaves fall, the twigs are seen to be jeweled with large rose-colored capsules that open to show orange-fleshed seeds. These specimens are so handicapped by hordes of sucking insects that they produce very little fruit but it is worth a search for the sake of its vibrant color scheme.

Cross the road at the traffic light and turn left, walking along the grass strip between road and bridle path towards a group of mature Turkey oaks, *Quercus cerris.* They present a graphic case book of proper and improper pruning.

As you approach the first tree from the south, you can see a healed wound on the left fork, about 4 feet above ground. In contrast, the upper surface of the right fork

154

shows an improperly trimmed stub which has rotted back and will result in a hollow trunk.

Walk around to the right, to the side of the tree nearest the bridle path, and you will see the process repeated. Instead of being cut flush with the trunk, the limb was cut with a protruding stub. The "heal"—a roll of new bark—is trying to cover the stub but decay has already entered the exposed wood and will work back into the trunk. When you move around to the north side of the tree, you will see even grosser neglect: two long-dead branches left to rot, and between them, a foot-long stub again showing decay. When limbs had to be removed with a hand saw, there may have been some temptation to cut through the narrow part of a branch rather than make the larger and more difficult flush cut, that is, even with the surface of the trunk. Now that workmen merely go *br-r-rt* with a chain saw, there's no excuse for lazy work that leaves stubs and invites decay.

Let's take a moment to consider the structure of a tree. All its life is concentrated in and immediately under the bark. Starting at the outside, the outer bark comes first. This is a layer of dead corky cells that protects the tree from injury by animals and fire, keeps the inner layers from losing moisture, and insulates against extremes of heat and cold. Next is the inner bark or phloem, the vital layer that conveys food manufactured by the leaves down to nourish the roots and encourage formation of feeding rootlets. When bark is damaged, roots are starved and the tree is deprived of part of its supply of water.

The most essential zone, the cambium layer, is almost invisible. It lies just inside the inner bark and is hardly more than a film of growth-controlling hormones called auxins. On its outer side, it promotes formation of new phloem cells. On the inner side, it builds new sapwood, the tissue that conducts water and nutrients from the roots to the upper parts of the tree.

155

The rest of the tree is dead, or at least inert. The innermost column, the heartwood, is made up of former sapwood rings, now without function except to support and strengthen the trunk. Though without life, the heartwood will not decay as long as it is covered by bark or—following injury or surgery—by a coat of protective wound dressing.

You can picture a tree, then, as a double-walled pipe with all its life, growth, and healing functions confined between the walls. A cut made close to this zone of activity will obviously have an optimum prospect of healing, while one made a distance from the living zone, as out on a dead branch, has no chance at all.

With this simplified diagram in mind, walk north to a pair of Turkey oaks to see how this theory is borne out in practice. As you face the right-hand tree, you will see a round scar on the trunk about 8 feet above ground. This is the result of a properly made cut, flush with the outer bark, in the area of maximum cell production. It has healed perfectly and is only noticeable because of the smooth texture of the young bark.

For comparison, look above the healed scar to a badly cut stub. If you stand back, you can see a broad band of heal extending from the growing zone of the trunk. This band of heal is broad enough so that it would by now have closed over the wound if the cut had been properly made. As it is, there is little chance that the heal can cover the stub before decay sets in.

If you are beginning to feel like a tree, look at the outer one of the pair, the one nearer the road, and shudder. Here is a shocking example of total neglect, with jagged, splintered stubs and a cavity already far advanced. If you have any lingering doubt about the need for a professional horticultural director and a staff of trained arboriculturists, I think this shameful exhibit will convince you.

Look across the bridle path to the border along the

reservoir where Japanese cherries have been planted so closely that they will not have room to develop. Here it is evident that money has been poured into a flashy display of high-maintenance garden subjects—"pretty little local effects," Olmsted would have called them— while the splendid old trees which are the backbone of the landscape are left to decay. The Park Department's scale of priorities is ripe for review.

As you retrace your steps, cross the road, take the left fork at lamp post #9011, and go down the steps towards the massive stone underpass. An Osage orange, *Maclura pomifera,* stands on each side of the bank only a few feet from the masonry. Neither bore fruit in 1969 and, if checked and found barren over a number of years, they may be presumed to be males.

As you walk through the underpass, you come out under a grove of cork trees. These are the common hairy-leafed variety, *Phellodendron amurense* var. *lavallei.* The second on the left, nearest the lamp post, is a female, as evidenced by its clusters of pea-sized black fruits. A fungus disease, especially noticeable in the gnarled, thickened branches overhanging the path on the right, has restricted growth and given the trees an unusually compressed, flat-topped appearance. They look so much like the acacias in the African Plains diorama in the Natural History Museum that it wouldn't be much of a surprise to come upon a giraffe browsing on their upper leaves.

Go up the steps and stop to admire a low-growing hawthorn in the angle of the path at the top. This is *Crataegus* x *prunifolium,* a hybrid with dull-surfaced crimson fruit and bronze-red autumn coloring. The leaf margins are finely toothed. Each half is an arc just short of being a semicircle. This is one of the commoner hawthorns in Central Park which you may want to be able to name. Another specimen, this time tree-like, touches lamp post #8903 across the path.

The walk that leads downhill towards the road is banked on both sides by a profusion of *Photinia villosa,* the shrub we admired near the start of the East Meadow tour. It is a splendidly rugged plant with an irregular, billowing habit that makes it entirely at home in a naturalistic setting. Its crop of red fruits, at their peak in mid-October, are so lavishly produced that they make a heartening display for visitors as well as providing food for migrating birds. These ample masses of photinia create a strong feeling of stability and assurance, an effect impossible to achieve with spotty, indecisive assortments.

Twenty feet to the right of a junction of paths is a female ailanthus, mantled in summer by great sprays of winged seed capsules of an uncommonly brilliant red. At a distance, the capsules look like flowers, showy enough to rival the royal poinciana of the tropics, and perhaps sufficient compensation for the nuisance of having to pull up myriads of unwanted seedlings.

A black cherry stands 15 feet south of the ailanthus, with a ginkgo 20 feet to its left. Beyond this grove, on the ridge to the right, are some straggly hemlocks, *Tsuga canadensis.* Hemlocks are fairly tolerant of polluted air but not of hot, dry, windswept situations. In the wild, hemlocks occur in the climax stage of a mature forest, on deep leafmold soil and in the dense shade required by their seedlings. They flourish especially on north-facing slopes where their roots are always shaded, cool, and moist. It is obvious that trees of a forest ecology can't survive on a parched hillside in full sun. If any pockets of leafmold remain in the Ramble or on the rocky slopes of the extreme northern section of the park, this would be the place to establish a hemlock grove. As natives of the region, hemlocks contribute to the authentic atmosphere of the woodland. In addition to the feathery grace of their fine-needled branches, hemlocks produce tiny cones which are prime attractors for chickadees and goldfinches.

In the original planting plan, West Drive from 79th Street north was planned for decorative effect in winter. Known as the Winter Drive, it was chiefly furnished with evergreens, both conifers and broad-leafed plants such as rhododendrons. Birches, red-twigged dogwood, and similar plants with colored bark, as well as berried trees such as mountain ash, hollies, and pyracantha were introduced for added cheer.

One by one, the firs, spruces, cedars, and many of the pines succumbed as air pollution reached an intolerable level. Aside from the few stalwarts that can endure city conditions—notably the Austrian, Himalayan, and Japanese black pines—most of the surviving tall conifers are deciduous: larch, golden larch, and bald cypress. The reason is this: deciduous trees shed their soiled leaves in fall and grow a fresh, clean crop each spring. Evergreens retain their leaves for more than one season and suffer a progressive build-up of soot. Like a dirty window-pane, a coating of soot blocks sunlight, the plant's source of energy. With the power supply diminished, manufacture of food in the leaves is curtailed. Roots in turn are deprived of nourishment; their intake of water dwindles; and ultimately the tree weakens and dies.

If the Winter Drive is to be replanted even in part, the choice of evergreens should be based on careful observation of types that actually exist in the city where their performance can be studied. It is regrettable that the list of tolerant, tall-growing evergreens is so limited but I think you will agree that a grove of hearty specimens is more pleasing than a wider variety of dying experiments.

Pass lamp post #8901 and pause as you reach the first bench. Across the lawn on the right is a large, exceptionally well-shaped ginkgo with wide-spreading branches and a handsome pedestal of buttress roots.

Seed-grown ginkgos show great variability of form. Some have sparse or irregular habit, often with one or more disproportionately long branches that impair the tree's balance. Nurseries are now propagating stock from superior individuals such as this one. Since ginkgos are slow growers, perhaps taking eighty years to attain the dignity of this mature tree, it is prudent to start with a named variety rather than an unpredictable seedling.

Ginkgos have long been thought immune to polluted city air but there is now disturbing evidence that they may be approaching their threshold of tolerance. Certainly the ginkgos along Central Park South are in sorry shape, though it is difficult to tell whether they are dying as a result of a lethal concentration of automotive fumes or of the brutal stubbing inflicted on them when branches were cut back nearly to the trunk. The slow death of trees by asphyxiation is not the most imperative argument for cleaning up our contaminated environment. We breath the same air.

South of the ginkgo, still on the slope, are two large saucer magnolias, *Magnolia* x *soulangeana,* with ash-gray bark disfigured by carved initials. In early May, the magnolias' naked branches are covered with great fleshy flowers of white and rose-pink, the floral counterpart of Ruben's full-blown nudes. Squint your eyes a bit and you can see the Sabine women making grandiose gestures of despair but very little effective resistance to capture.

Saucer magnolias are so opulent, so obviously exotic, that they make fitting ornaments for structures of great elegance and formality. They are admirably suited to the garden of the Frick Collection and, as they once appeared, in plantings enclosed by the curving wings of the Central Park Terrace. However, Peet shows a good number of saucer magnolias in the Ramble! It's hard to reconcile the use of these ostentatious hybrids with Olmsted's clear direction to produce "a much more natural wild character" in the Ramble. The growth of the woods has canceled this lapse of taste by shading the magnolias out of existence.

Return to the path and stop just north of the tall lamp post #8802, under a female ginkgo at the roadside, By mid-October, the fruit ripens to a pinkish tan color and starts to drop, making an ill-smelling and dangerously slippery mess on the pavement—proof of the advisability of planting only male ginkgos near footpaths.

Only the fleshy covering of the fruit is offensive. The nut is prized as a delicacy by Orientals. For exact recipes, look up two sumptuously illustrated *Time & Life* books, one on Chinese, one on Japanese cooking. A dish for the autumn season—a combination of shrimp, chicken, mushrooms, and ginkgo nuts cooked on a bed of salt overlaid with pine needles—is so beautifully pictured that you can almost smell its tangy aroma. Ginkgo nuts, boiled, seasoned with salt and sugar and threaded in pairs on twin pine needles, are an item of the ceremonial first meal of the new year. For less formal autumn gatherings, the nuts are roasted over a hibachi and eaten hot.

I've never dared to touch the nuts: according to many authorities, the juice of the outer coating is irritating to the skin and can cause inflammation similar to that from poison ivy. I was astonished, therefore, to come upon an elderly Chinese couple gathering ginkgo nuts, stripping off the slimy pulp with bare fingers, and dropping the kernels into two bulging plastic bags.

I asked the wife how she used the nuts in cooking but she had no English and could only bow and smile. The husband politely did his best with words—"soup. . . chicken"—and then demonstrated, first washing a nut in pantomime, then cracking its brittle shell under his foot. The kernel he offered me was enclosed in a tough

161

skin. Inside this was a crisp, bright green nut, looking and tasting exactly like a raw pea.

It may be that the irritant in the outer flesh is less potent after frost. Nevertheless, I plan to wear rubber gloves when I go out to gather ginkgo nuts next fall.

Ginkgos are among the most ancient of flowering plants, related to tree ferns, cycads, and conifers through similarities in their system of reproduction. Except that ginkgo pollen produces a motile (swimming) sperm cell, as do ferns and cycads, the details are too abstruse for a non-technical discussion. However, you can easily note a feature common to ginkgos, larches, and golden larch: the leaves—except for those on fast-growing terminal shoots—are borne on a short spur, not directly on the twig.

Across the road is a European birch, *Betula pendula,* with supple, gracefully dipping branches. This species is able to do quite satisfactorily under city conditions and to survive the hot summers that quickly kill off our northern paper birch.

Below the birch, nearer the road, are three recently planted young evergreens. The two to the left are *Cryptomeria japonica,* a tree that grows to mammoth size in Japan but is near the borderline of hardiness in this region. The blue-tinged sapling on the right is *Cedrus atlantica glauca,* the blue cedar of the Atlas Mountains of North Africa. This again is doubtfully hardy. There are good specimens in a sheltered spot in the Brooklyn Botanic Garden, warmer than Central Park because of its promimity to the ocean. This windswept gully bordering a road where the trees receive a maximum concentration of exhaust fumes seems unlikely to prove congenial.

Walk on past lamp post #8711 to the far end of the grassy triangle. The footpath is flanked by two maples. On the left is a red-leafed Schwedler maple, *Acer platanoides* var. *schwedleri,* which we first saw at the south end of Conservatory Water. This is a variety of Norway maple, as you can confirm by comparing it with the normal, green-leafed specimen on the right of the path. The tight, finely grooved bark and horizontally aligned key fruits are identical in form; leaves and fruits differ only in color.

Turn right at the end of the triangle and start back towards Central Park West. Just beyond the point where two paths join, a pair of *Sophora japonica* flank the walk. These trees have green-barked twigs and pinnately compound leaves with oval leaflets. Sophoras are conspicuous until late autumn for their dangling green pods, and even later for their foliage which remains green long after most trees are bare.

Flowers of the sophora are used in the Orient to produce a yellow dye. Peet states that the name sophora derives from the Arabic *zapharan,* or saffron, also important as a dye. I confess to preferring this sensible explanation to the meaningless common names of Pagoda or Scholar Tree but I have not found any other authority to support Peet's ingenious theory.

The pine in the semicircle of blocks ahead on the right is the reliable Austrian pine. The bark, patterned with large light-colored plates separated by dark crevices, is a quick key to identification. As a check, look for long needles, two to a bundle and with a pronounced twist.

The shrubs behind the railing on both sides are Washinton thorns, *Crataegus phaenopyrum,* very widely used and one of the easiest species to identify. In early June the shrubs bear fairly showy white flowers with a most unpleasant wet-dog odor. These are followed by clusters of small fruits, light yellow at first, showing red cheeks near the end of September, then ripening to bright red. The fruits persist long after the leaves have fallen. The thickets of red-berried shrubs you see along parkways in winter are probably Washington thorns.

The Winter Drive

When the shrubs are in leaf, you can study the vein pattern. In most thorns, the veins extend only to the tips of the lobes. The distinguishing mark of the Washington thorn is that some of its veins end at the sinus, the hollow between the lobes. If you think this is a finicky distinction, I heartily agree, and urge you to enjoy your walks in the park even if you can't tell one hawthorn from another.

"We live in an era when almost everything man does is hostile to nature. Evidences of this hostility surround us: polluted air, polluted water, excess noise, rubbish and litter and dishevelment, tension in the cities, and a flagrant and ruthless assault of man upon the landscape and upon life itself.

"Suddenly in a brief half century, man has alienated himself from his natural world, has become hostile to it, and as a consequence, has become seriously dehumanized. The crises in our cities are but a symptom of a deeply disturbed environment of man."

Dr. Joseph J. Shomon, 1968
Director: Audubon Nature Centers

164

XI

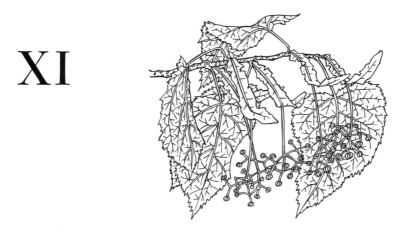

THE ROAD TO
TANNER'S SPRING

86th Street and
Central Park West

THIS is a connoisseur's walk, saved for last like the
icing on a cake. You will have a first view of some startling
rarities including what may be the last natural spring on
the island of Manhattan. Since repetition is the best way
to fix distinguishing marks in memory, there is a final
review of native oaks. If you have oaks well in hand, you
can tick them off without referring to the description.
Once again, you'll find it convenient to read the explana-
tory material before you start out.

Enter the park through a gap in the wall about 50 feet

south of the 86th Street transverse. The first sizable tree on the right, with roots exposed by erosion, has opposite branches and leaflets of nearly uniform size. The leaflets are hairless, green on both sides, and set directly on the main stalk or on short, winged stalks. This is the mark of the green ash, *Fraxinus pennsylvanica* var. *subintegerrima*. To review, the white ash has leaflets with white or pale undersides and long, usually wingless leafstalks. The red ash, as we shall see near the end of this tour, has downy shoots and leaflets heavily furred on the underside.

A word on shifting fashions in nomenclature: botanists lean towards being either Lumpers or Splitters. Splitters like to term each slight variation a separate species. Lumpers tend to select one form as the species and describe slightly differing forms as varieties. At present the Lumpers seem to be ascendant. The red (hairy) and green (hairless) ashes were once treated as separate species, but so many intermediate forms occur that the distinction becomes blurred. The red ash is now considered the type and the green ash a variety of it. The same change has recently been made with cork trees. You may have thought of taxonomy as a cut-and-dried science. It is in fact a continual round of pussy-wants-a-corner, with each revision touching off a series of changes. As for the new varietal name *subintegerrima*, it translates roughly as "almost most entire margined," which seems an unnecessarily devious way of arriving at "nearly toothless."

As you walk forward into the park, look up the slope to the right where an Austrian pine, *Pinus nigra*, stands like a sentinal on the hilltop. The characteristic bark pattern of light-colored plates is well displayed on this specimen.

The screen planting which should shut out the traffic on the transverse road has entirely disappeared. According to Olmsted's directions, the screens were composed of spruces, shown in old photographs as a high, dense wall

166

which shut out all view of traffic and muffled its noise. Spruces have long since succumbed to contaminated air but more tolerant trees and shrubs would serve quite as well. Transverse roads are a marvelously ingenious device for keeping commercial traffic out of park roads but their purpose is defeated unless vehicles are screened from sight and hearing of park visitors.

Beyond the end of the rock outcrop, behind lamp post #8537, is a four-trunked black cherry, *Prunus serotina,* with fingerlike clusters of small white flowers and sprays of shining black fruit. The cherries have a bracing, bitter-sweet flavor when ripe and are invaluable food for wild birds. The picturesque, low branching habit of black cherries make them excellent subjects for a natural landscape.

Beyond the black cherry, the next large tree, with its trunk close to the right side of the path, is a swamp white oak, *Quercus bicolor.* There is another behind it close to the playground fence which displays the typical drooping branch pattern. This is also characteristic of the pin oak, but if you remember that pin oaks have sharp, needle-pointed lobes and white oaks have rounded leaf margins, you will not be confused. The swamp white oak leaf is not so deeply cut as the white oak's, and tends to broaden towards the tip instead of tapering. The bark is rough and medium gray, darker than a white oak's and peeling in coarse, not papery, flakes.

Twenty feet beyond lamp post #8535, a small tree, only about 6 inches in diameter, is being shaded to death. It is a black oak, *Q. velutina,* distinguished by broad, shining leaves and—bearing out its name *velutina* (velvety)—downy leafstalks and buds matted with gray hairs. This luckless tree was planted under a huge, blanketing pin oak without regard for sunlight, growing room, or waste of taxpayers' money.

167

Pin oaks, greatly overplanted in Central Park, are too familiar to need description. Let's look for more interesting subjects. Turn right before you reach the pin oak and walk on the grass towards the closed gates in the playground fence. To the right of the gates is a nannyberry, *Viburnum lentago,* another native member of this invaluable genus. The nannyberry's round black fruits are eaten by birds as soon as they ripen. Other distinguishing marks are more enduring. The majority of viburnums have oval leaves but the tips of the nannyberry's are drawn into long tapering points. Examine the leafstalks with your hand lens: you will find near the base of the leaf some toothed wings like tiny cockscombs. Flower buds are long and slender except for a bulge in the middle, suggesting a snake that has swallowed an egg in the shell.

On the left as you face the gate are three *Viburnum prunifolium,* the largest one limbed up and showing its bark pattern of small, lizard-scale plates much like a dogwood's. The similarity of the bark will cause no confusion if you remember that *V. prunifolium* leaves have veins that branch out to the margins in fishbone pattern, while those of the dogwoods follow the curve of the border, avoiding the margin and meeting at or near the tip.

Now return to the path and continue into the park. The next tree on the right beyond the large pin oak is a Norway maple, and across the path from the maple is a small red oak, *Quercus rubra.* Look first for red leafstalks and then, for certainty, the reddish or chestnut-brown buds, hairless except for a fringe at the extreme tip of the bud scales.

Ten feet before the end of the fence on the left is a two-trunked green ash with unusually deeply ridged, irregularly broken bark. A check of stalkless leaflets with hairless undersides will confirm the identification.

Just in line with the end of the fence, still on the left,

is a small Turkey oak, *Q. cerris.* This specimen is too young to show more than a hint of its mature bark pattern but the long acorns in fringed cups and the litter of unfertile female flowers on the ground are sufficient clues.

Beyond #9531 is a European hornbeam, 2 feet from the path on the left, with another behind it at the bottom of the slope. When fruit is present, you'll have no difficulty in recognizing the European hornbeam's 1½ inch, round-tipped bracts. If you must depend on buds, remember that buds of the European hornbeam are ¼ inch in length, and those of the American only ⅛ inch.

As you come to the curve of the path, you will see a huge, sprawling paulownia, *P. tomentosa,* close by on the left. If you recall the giant specimen beside the upper level of the Terrace, you will recognize the tree in any season by its large, heart-shaped, opposite leaves; violet tubular flowers; upright clusters of tan, felt-covered buds; and pecan-shaped fruit capsules. As you take the path to the right, look back to see how handsomely the light-colored buds are displayed on the sloping branches.

Across the path from the paulownia is a large hackberry with a profusion of witches' brooms and many broken branches. Heavily infested hackberries are especially vulnerable to snow damage, as the brooms catch and hold masses of snow that would slide harmlessly off normal twigs.

If you stop at lamp post #8529 and look somewhat to its left towards the playground fence, you will see a beautiful golden larch, *Pseudolarix amabilis.* As the prefix *pseudo* (false or imitation) implies, the golden larch is not a true larch. The chief difference is in the cones.

The cones of true larches, like those of pines, are woody and persistent. As they ripen, the scales draw apart and release the seeds but the cones themselves remain intact. If you will visualize the pine cones used in Christmas

169

decorations, you will recall that their scales are separated and reflexed almost like flower petals but are still quite solidly attached to the central spine.

In the golden larch, the large, fleshy cones fall apart as they ripen, shedding seeds and scales together. If you are fortunate enough to find a cone on the ground, take it home, let it dry, and watch how it drops into pieces. As a scale falls off, it uncovers two winged seeds, cupped like the blade of a pinwheel and spinning like a whirligig when tossed into the air.

Cones of the pseudolarix may be seen near the top of the tree. In early summer, the tobacco-brown tassels of male flowers are conspicuous on the lower branches. This placement (seen also in pines, alders, birches, and other wind-pollinated trees) is an ingenious device to avoid self-pollination. Pollen is not likely to be lifted straight up in the air to the female flowers of the same tree. Instead, it is swept away to the cones of other trees in the grove.

Needles of true larches and pseudolarix are borne on short, stubby spurs—as are ginkgo leaves, if you recall. Larches have their needles in stiff shaving-brush tufts. Those of the pseudolarix are arranging in whorls, making a saucer of radiating needles.

After returning to the path, you will see on the right a paulownia and then an Austrian pine which you will recognize by its long, paired, twisted needles. This specimen has a dead stub which should be cut flush with the trunk so that it can heal.

At this point, leave the footpath and walk to the right. It's always a bit difficult to navigate when trees must substitute for numbered lamp posts. As a general guide, the route goes south along the playground fence.

Ten feet beyond the Austrian pine is a Scots pine, *Pinus sylvestris,* with conspicuous red-orange bark on the upper branches. The needles are short, gray-green,

and carried in bundles of two. A flourishing Scots pine has an open, irregular head that displays its colorful bark with striking effect. Since most pines are a uniformly somber green, it is most regrettable that this bright-hued species has apparently reached the limit of its tolerance of contaminated air. As I've said earlier, a sooty coating on leaves reduces their capacity to manufacture food. If you take a look at your ankles after just one day's walk in the park, you'll have an idea of what city plants must endure.

As you continue walking towards the fence, you come to a good-sized oak with leaves about the size of a red oak's but with deeper and wider sinuses, often semicircular in outline. This is a scarlet oak, *Quercus coccinea,* thought by some botanists to be a natural hybrid between pin and red oaks. The drooping branches of this specimen certainly suggest a measure of pin oak blood. However, if you turn a leaf over, you will see that its underside is shiny, a feature that immediately distinguishes the scarlet oak from pin, red and black oaks.

Scarlet oak acorn cups are quite deep, enclosing the nut for more than half its length. The coarse scales that cover the cup are close fitting, not jutting like those of black oaks.

As you follow around the fence to the south, you come upon a *Viburnum prunifolium* which seems at first glance to have purple flowers and scarlet berries. These in fact belong to bittersweet nightshade, *Solanum dulcamara,* a woody vine related to peppers, tomatoes, potatoes, and the poisonous *Datura stramonium,* or Jimson weed. Except for their purple color, the flowers with reflexed petals and a conelike dart of stamens are very like those of tomatoes. Authorities differ about the toxic effect of the temptingly juicy, clear red berries. Considering the nightshade's dubious relatives, I have no inclination to put the theories to practical test. Because of its small, deeply cut leaves

172

and moderate growth, the nightshade will not harm the viburnum as would a smothering vine like wild grape or Japanese honeysuckle.

Next in line along the fence are a *Viburnum prunifolium* and a young Turkey oak locked in a death struggle. You can speculate on which came first and which is the invader. Did a bird perch on the oak and drop viburnum seeds, or did a jay or squirrel bury an acorn under the virburnum? At this time, both contestants seem to be holding their own. It will be interesting to see whether the truce continues or whether the oak will eventually shade the viburnum to death.

On the left side of the earth path, opposite the competitors, is a shiny-leafed tree with shallowly ridged bark. This is a white mulberry, *Morus alba*. The tint of orange in bark crevices and on the exposed root recall the more strongly colored bark of the related Osage orange. A well-fruited mulberry is a prime attractor of birds— perhaps the only reason for tolerating this messy and invasive tree.

Walk southwest between the mulberry and an Austrian pine to a small, black-barked tree reaching for the light. At first sight of its round lobes, auricles, and very short leafstalks, I took it for an English oak, *Quercus robur*. However, its auricles didn't seem pronounced enough and there was something wrong with the proportion of the leaf. As always when in doubt, I submitted a sample to George Kalmbacher.

George whipped out his hand lens, examined the underside of several leaves, and found them covered with stellate (split) hairs. This is a characteristic of another English oak, *Q. petraea*. *Robur* has simple hairs, if any. *Petraea*, on the other hand, has no auricles but does have a longish leafstalk. Since this tree combines the stellate hairs of *petraea* with the auricles and short leafstalks of *robur*, it was declared to be a hybrid of the two, *Q* x

173

rosacea—a common occurrence in England where the parent species grow in the same area but exceedingly rare in this country. For this reason, the little tree should be given every encouragement: a good feeding and—more important—relief from crowding by the intruding branches of commoner trees, the mulberry and a black cherry. Rescuing this unique hybrid oak is a worthy project for the Friends of Central Park in 1970.

Walk south between the lamp post and the last bench, cross the path, and head for the smooth, sloping rock at the foot of the rise. The twisting tree with its roots in a rock crevice is a paper mulberry, *Broussonetia papyrifera*. The young leaves are deliciously velvety and of a singularly luminous tender green. As with the white mulberry, the leaves show great variation in form. Some mimic the mitten-lobes of sassafras. Others with five lobes resemble fig leaves, another clue, as figs also belong to the mulberry family. The paper mulberry, an Asian tree, is a rampant weed, so invasive that it can only be tolerated in rough places such as this rocky bank.

When you return to the path, walk towards Central Park West. At lamp post #8505, turn left into the little tree-framed meadow, by now familiar to you as one of Olmsted's most charming devices for creating a secluded country retreat in the midst of the city.

A European beech stands as gatepost on the right, and is echoed by others along the edge of the road. All of these have been limbed too high to show their characteristic habit or to serve as effectual screens. Untreated wounds on the trunk are beginning to decay and should have prompt treatment.

As you stand on the top of the rise, you will see on the right a two-trunked European hornbeam with branches dipping to the ground on the meadow side to make a beautiful and functional barrier. The gaps on either side should be closed with comparable ground-sweeping trees

174

and shrubs to insulate the meadow from the disturbing sight and sound of automobile traffic.

As you look south into the meadow, you have an opportunity to test how well you have assimilated Olmsted's principles of park design. Remembering his directions on how to create "the broadest effects of light and shade. . . and the impression of great space and freedom," can you pick out the flaw that mars the picture? Yes, it's the two stiff pin oaks standing in the center. They interrupt the flowing contour of the grass and add nothing of interest. Blank them out with your hand or mentally transplant them to the sparse border on the east and you will see how the meadow enlarges. Olmsted's central purpose and his directions for carrying out his concept are clear, detailed, and easily grasped. It is difficult to understand how the caretakers of his park could fail to comprehend them.

Diagonally to the left, in the direction of the rock outcrop near West Drive, are two black oaks, *Quercus velutina*. Their broad, solid-looking leaves are at the opposite extreme from the pin oak's small, deeply cut foliage. These trees show typical black oak bark with a pattern of small, rough plates. Leafstalks and buds are downy. Acorn cups are deep and coarsely scaled, with the tips of the scales jutting out from the surface.

Once basic features are established, slight deviations can be taken in stride. The tree on the left has slightly cupped leaves with a puckered surface, possibly the result of a fungus infection. The right-hand one has reddish leafstalks, supposedly a trait of the red oak. To be sure, this is the only black oak with red leafstalks I've found in the park. Still, the exception proves that superficial clues are not wholly reliable. They merely offer a hint of what to look for next.

The two black oaks would have been better planted nearer the edge of the meadow. As it is, their stiff isolation could be relieved with a planting of understory trees and shrubs extending back to the rocks and linking the oaks with the border planting.

If you now follow the striations of the rock to the right, you will find two enormous horsechestnuts, *Aesculus hippocastanum,* near the access road. This is a monumental tree: all its details—massive trunk and branches, thick shoots, fat buds, huge palmate leaves, and 18 inch flower clusters—are designed on a heroic scale. The horsechestnut is at its best at the edge of a woodland where soil is cool and moist. Exposure to drying heat, especially when doubled by reflection from a pavement or roadway, turns the leaves of horsechestnuts rusty brown from leaf scorch by midsummer. Because of its substantial head, the horsechestnut is an ideal choice to strengthen flimsy border plantings.

The next large tree as you approach the junction of the roads is an American linden, *Tilia americana,* with leaves as much as 8 inches long and fruiting bracts only a fraction shorter. In youth the American linden is a hobbledehoy: it is only in maturity that it grows up to its leaves. In the South it is called basswood or bee tree, the latter name referring to the strongly flavored, fragrant honey derived from its flowers. This is the healthiest specimen I have seen in the park. As yet it shows no injury from the disastrous increase in air pollution that is killing off other American lindens in the city.

Cross the road to your right. On the far side, by lamp post #8303, is a red oak, *Quercus rubra,* which shows the characteristic broad, pale gray ribbons of smooth bark on the upper trunk. With your hand lens, study the beautiful gradation of color on the bud scales: amber brown at the base, darkening to chestnut at the tip. The scales are hairier than is typical but the hairs are brown, not gray, so there is no chance of confusing this with a black oak.

176

The Road to Tanner's Spring

This is a well formed tree and, as the only one of consequence in the area, should be given particular care. Instead, it is already endangered by rotting stubs, the mark of ignorant or slovenly workmanship.

Neglect of trees is no recent phenomenon. In 1907, Samuel Parsons, Jr. sternly warned the Park Board:

> "Probably in another twenty years, unless comparatively large sums of money and great intelligence are used by those dealing with the restoration of the New York parks, they will become disgraceful wastes. . . . Even today one can readily see by the briefest examination that the dead and dying trees are numerous, that soil has been unduly washed away from around their roots, that in some places they are crowded and need thinning out. . . ."

In 1902, a scholarly report on soils and similar basic problems recommends "careful and competent pruning and protection of cut surfaces." In the same pamphlet, the Central Park Restoration Committee of the Parks and Playgrounds Association reports that "Central Park is rich in rare and valuable trees, but they are as a whole suffering from lack of scientific pruning, of competent tree surgery, and erosions about the roots, exposing them to the sun, bruising and all sorts of injury." This was written in 1910 and, along with subsequent surveys such as the Merkel Report, has been totally ignored.

Drawing on his nearly thirty years' experience as Superintendent of Parks, Landscape Architect, and Park Commissioner, Parsons concluded: "All the troubles of the New York Park Department have arisen from failure to understand the value of expert advice." If the advice of outside experts has been brushed aside for sixty years, while the condition of the park steadily deteriorates, isn't it time to put experts in charge?

Turn south and walk along the roadside, passing a triangular YIELD sign with a Washington thorn at its elbow. At the next tall lamp post, turn right and walk to the edge of the woods. The little umbrella-headed evergreen tree is *Buxus sempervirens,* the boxwood familiar in the gardens of the Middle South. The pale gray, finely checkered bark is attractive but the trunk is marred by cuts whose exposed wood, unprotected by wound dressing, is drying and cracking. The generally hardier Japanese hollies are often mistaken for boxwood but hollies have alternate leaves while those of boxwood are opposite.

Ten feet behind the boxwood and slightly to its left is a cork tree, *Phellodendron amurense* var. *amurense,* the uncommon hairless type. This specimen is a female tree. It would be interesting to sow some of the seeds to find out whether the seedlings have hairless leaves or whether they take after the vastly predominant hairy forms, one of which may have been the pollen parent.

If you walk a little way into the woods, somewhat southwest of the cork tree, you will find a tiny spring and thread-sized brook. This is Tanner's Spring, named for a Dr. Henry S. Tanner who, in the summer of 1880, set himself to fast for forty days and forty nights. No reason is given, but the duration of the ordeal suggests that Dr. Tanner may have been trying to prove the veracity of a Bible story. At first he intended to abstain from water as well as food but—fortunately for him—thirst overcame his resolution. By this time his outraged stomach rejected water from all conventional sources—Croton, bottled, and mineral. Only water from the Central Park spring was acceptable, and with its help, the doctor was able to finish his self-imposed test. The legend quite naturally arose that the water of the spring contained some magically concentrated nutrients. Actually it is reported to be very pure and would be potable if you could get the water directly from the source. As it is, the open box into which the water now flows exposes it to contamination, particularly from the pigeons that flock to this area.

178

Continue downhill and cross the bridle path at the big rock. Continue around it to the right beside a line of Norway maples, planted in the street tree style that Olmsted deplored. After you pass lamp post #8117, count off three Norway maples. The fourth tree, just short of #8009, is a Japanese painted maple, *Acer mono*, an exceedingly rare maple that somehow strayed into a nursery row and was accidentally included in a shipment of common trees.

The painted maple is an elegant species, dainty and refined in all its details. The leaves are smaller than those of the Norway maple, brighter green, and with the three bottom lobes equal in size and widely spaced. The bark is notably beautiful: smooth pale gray with stripes of orange in the shallow crevices. Remember this pattern: we shall see it again soon on a totally unrelated tree.

Directly across the path from the painted maple are two enormous silver maples, *Acer saccharinum*. You may recall the deeply cut leaves and frosted undersides, first seen at the start of the East Meadow tour. The sap is sweet, as indicated by the name *saccharinum*, but its flow is less abundant than that of the sugar maple, *A. saccharum*. In the Middle West, where the heat-intolerant sugar maple doesn't thrive, farmers turned to the silver maple for their sweetener—perhaps they still do—but the yield is too small to make it commercially profitable.

Cross the bridle path and walk up the little rocky rise on your right. On top of the over-trampled hill is a tree with exposed roots spidering out in all directions. It has pinnately compound leaves, with the three terminal leaflets markedly larger than the basal ones. This is the distinguishing mark of hickories, and this hickory the easiest to identify: the bitternut, *Carya cordiformis*. Study the end buds under your hand lens: they are bright golden yellow with a powdery finish. The paired bud scales,

179

instead of overlapping in the conventional way, lie parallel with their edges just meeting, rather like the jaws of a dolphin. You can, if you want, count the leaflets—usually seven—and note the ridges on the thin husk of the nut. None of this is really needed, however, if you can reach a branch and examine a bud with its coating of gold dust.

This hickory is young enough to retain its beautifully colored juvenile bark: pale gray on the rounded ridges, pinkish orange between—a singular resemblance to the Japanese painted maple we have just seen.

As you continue north over the rise, notice on your left at the edge of the path a superb two-trunked sweet gum, *Liquidambar styraciflua*, the tree notable for its star-shaped leaves and magnificent autumn coloring. Both its names refer to its pungent sap, sweet-smelling when dried and burned.

In the Middle Ages, when sanitation was unknown, bad smells were correctly associated with disease, attributed to evil spirits. If devils were attracted by bad smells, it was reasoned, they could be banished by good smells. Incense was accordingly burned in churches and sickrooms to keep the forces of evil at bay, while scented herbs and resins were in demand for use in medicines. One of the scarce and costly resins—variously known as liquidambar, balm, balsam, and storax—came from a sweet gum, *L. orientalis*, collected chiefly in Turkey. A new source of sweet gum resin, of excellent quality and unlimited quantity, was one of the rewards of the treasure-seekers who explored the American wilderness.

The very large tree standing alone on the slope across the path is a red ash, *Fraxinus pennsylvanica* var. *pennsylvanica*, not previously seen on these tours. As you recall, the hairless green ash is a variety of this species. This tree is too high branched to permit examining leaves but there is a row of saplings, presumably seedlings of the large tree, growing along the edge of a low rock shelf on the left side of the path. If you climb the rocks, you can easily grasp a branch. The underside of the leaves, their winged stalks, and the young shoots are all densely covered with fine velvety down. You may remember that the leaflets of the white ash are hairy along the veins on the underside, not over the entire surface, while leafstalks and shoots are hairless. For a final check, look at the leaf scar: it is a semicircle or shield, with only a slight indentation at the top for the bud. For comparison, the leaf scar of the white ash is a wide crescent, with the bud set well down between its points.

If you have an exceptional memory, you may recall the problem ash near Conservatory Water (p. 38) which had white ash leaf scars and pubescence but leaflets of extraordinarily heavy texture on winged leaf stalks, and bark broken into short V's. You may recognize some of these characteristics in the red ash, and join the controversy over the possible hybrid nature of the Conservatory Water enigma.

During the winter, you can practice tree recognition by studying the superlative dioramas in the American Museum of Natural History, where dogwood and silverbell are always in flower and autumn foliage never fades. Perhaps more important, you can see plants in their natural ecological groupings. The setting for the white-tail deer is beside a pond at Bear Mountain. Red maple and sour gum frame the view, with the native witch-hazel in flower at the left and fallen white oak leaves on the ground. On the painted background, *Clethra alnifolia* is in late bloom; sassafras leaves add yellow and apricot tones; and at the water's edge, highbush blueberries glow in their red autumn dress. This natural association can serve as a model for replanting the barren shores of the Lake and Pool and for the banks of the

181

Gill in the Ramble which Olmsted planned as a preserve of native plants in a woodland setting.

The oak-hickory forest, with its leafmold carpet and vigorous undergrowth of intermediate trees, saplings, and seedlings, sets a pattern for the wooded hills at the northern end of the park.

As this book goes to press, there is heartening news that the Museum will take an active role in the rehabilitation of the city's parks and in its nature study program. Dr. James A. Oliver has been appointed Environmental Consultant to the Park Department. His duties will include advising on specific problems such as checking erosion caused by the stripping of banks in Prospect Park and by heedless cutting of trails in Inwood Park. In addition to expanding existing nature study centers such as High Rock in Staten Island, Dr. Oliver will develop educational programs in city parks. To this end, he intends to restore the remaining wild areas—the Ramble and northern section of Central Park, and the Ravine in Prospect Park, among others—to serve as outdoor classrooms for the city's school children.

The appointment of a scientist of Dr. Oliver's stature is a tremendous advance, as it brings technical competence and experience in public education into the fight for the city's survival. Dr. Oliver is keenly aware that the role of ecologist is so vast and so crucial that it can only be filled on a full time basis. His most vital assignment is to choose a central environmental officer to supervise the city's parks and wildlife refuges. By the time you start following these tours, a trained ecologist may already have walked the trails and made plans to restore the park to its original luxuriant beauty.

APRIL 1970

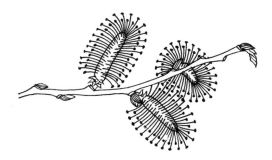

INDEX

Index

188

Index

Designed by Charles Farrell.
Composed in Linotype Caledonia, with display in Bulmer,
by Port City Press, Inc., Baltimore, Maryland.
Lithographed on Mohawk Laid Book and bound by
Malloy Lithographing Inc., Ann Arbor, Michigan.